AF674747

GST in India

GST IN INDIA

Simple Tax in a Complex Federal System

Pinaki Chakraborty

Orient BlackSwan

GST IN INDIA: SIMPLE TAX IN A COMPLEX FEDERAL SYSTEM

ORIENT BLACKSWAN PRIVATE LIMITED

Registered Office
3-6-752 Himayatnagar, Hyderabad 500 029, Telangana, India
e-mail: centraloffice@orientblackswan.com

Other Offices
Bangalore, Bhopal, Chennai, Guwahati,
Hyderabad, Jaipur, Kolkata, Lucknow, Mumbai,
New Delhi, Noida, Patna, Visakhapatnam

© Orient Blackswan Private Limited 2019
First published by Orient BlackSwan in 2019

ISBN 978-93-5287-689-1

030133

Typeset in
Minion Pro 11/13
by Shine Graphics, Delhi

Printed in India at
Akash Press, New Delhi

Published by
Orient Blackswan Private Limited
3-6-752, Himayatnagar Hyderabad 500 029, Telangana, India
e-mail: info@orientblackswan.com

For

I. S. Gulati and Thomas Isaac

Contents

Tables, Figures and Boxes

TABLES

Figures

Boxes

Abbreviations

BE	budget estimate
CAG	Comptroller and Auditor General of India
CBEC	Central Board of Excise and Customs
CBIC	Central Board of Indirect Taxes and Customs (previously, CBEC)
CENVAT	Central value-added tax
CFI	Consolidated Fund of India
CGA	Controller General of Accounts
CGST	Central goods and services tax
CII	Confederation of Indian Industry
CKD	completely knocked down
CPI	Consumer Price Index
CST	central sales tax
CVD	countervailing duty
EAC	East African Community
EEC	Eurasian Economic Space
EPFO	Employees' Provident Fund Organisation
ESIC	Employees' State Insurance Corporation
FRBM	Fiscal Responsibility and Budget Management Act, 2003
GST	Goods and Services Tax
GSTN	Goods and Services Tax Network
GDP	gross domestic product
GSP	GST Suvidha Provider
GVA	gross value added
HSN	Harmonised System Nomenclature
IGST	integrated goods and services tax
IMF	International Monetary Fund
ITC	input tax credit
MODVAT	modified value-added tax
NCAER	National Council of Applied Economic Research

NCEUS	National Commission for Enterprises in the Unorganised Sector
NDA	National Democratic Alliance
NIC	National Informatics Centre
NIPFP	National Institute of Public Finance and Policy
NSC	National Statistical Commission
NSSO	National Sample Survey Office
OECD	Organisation for Economic Co-operation and Development
PIB	Press Information Bureau
RBI	Reserve Bank of India
RNR	revenue neutral rate
RST	retail sales tax
SAD	special additional duty
SBI	State Bank of India
SEZ	Special Economic Zone
SGST	state goods and services tax
SHEC	Secondary and Higher Education Cess
UNCTAD	United Nations Conference on Trade and Development
UTGST	Union Territory GST
VAT	value-added tax

Preface and Acknowledgements

The introduction of the goods and services tax (GST) has been hailed as the most important tax reform in India since independence. The sheer scale and dimension of this reform deserve credit. The introduction of GST required amendments to the Constitution of India to enable the Union and 29 state governments to levy tax on a common tax base. This common base merged production and consumption taxes together. The idea was to simplify the tax system and tax at the point of consumption, thus avoiding distortionary effects of production and origin-based taxation. While the impact of GST is far-reaching, its effect on the functioning of the economy and various economic agents—producers, distributors and consumers—will only be known in the medium to long term, when we have meaningful data to understand its impact. The analysis in this book is indicative, commenting on the direction of reform and the challenges ahead. The book also undertakes an analysis of the revenue impact of GST in the Indian federal system.

After the introduction of GST on 1 July 2017, I was approached by Nilanjana Majumdar of Orient BlackSwan to write a non-technical book on the topic. I happily agreed to the proposal. Making sense of a tax that had just been introduced and was going through frequent changes, and writing a book on it was challenging. In the absence of any meaningful data, I tried to follow regular updates on GST from various sources, particularly the minutes of various GST Council meetings from the Press Information Bureau press releases. Analysing the minutes of the meetings gave me a sense that although India started with multiple rates and various kinds of differentiated tax rates across product and commodity groups, it was soon realised that course correction would be necessary. Efforts are on to reduce the number of goods in the highest tax bracket and to simplify the tax design. I am convinced that GST today is a better version of what it was on 1 July 2017. It is hoped that the system stabilises and we have an indirect tax system that is simple, transparent and non-distortionary.

Given my training and its associated biases, I am not entirely sure how successfully I have been able to write a non-technical book. This book is a combination of technical analysis and simple narrative, explaining various facets of GST and the rationale for its introduction in India. The objective is to understand why GST was introduced and what its impacts are. The book also provides a historical analysis to understand the complexity of tax reforms in a federal system. It reflects on various challenges and possibilities to improve the system to achieve the objective of simplicity, transparency and neutrality in the implementation of GST. The book also reflects on what impedes the development of a common market and the idea of 'one nation, one tax'.

In this endeavour, I have been supported by two young colleagues of mine, Shatakshi Garg and Shubham Gupta. Shatakshi did painstaking data analysis and helped me immensely in drafting Chapter 4. Shubham prepared short notes on various aspects of GST and a comprehensive review of literature. I am immensely indebted to these two young and dynamic researchers. I have greatly benefitted from various discussions on GST at the NIPFP and in the Fourteenth Finance Commission. I would particularly like to acknowledge the understanding I gained through recent discussions with Dr Y. V. Reddy, Dr M. Govind Rao, Mr A. M. Jha and Dr R. Kavita Rao.

I am grateful to an anonymous referee for very valuable comments, and to Nilanjana Majumdar at Orient BlackSwan for the follow-ups and excellent coordination. Nilanjana's support and coordination have been critical in the publication of this book. I have received unstinted support from my wife Lekha and son Shubhamaditya. I am grateful to both of them. Lekha also highlighted certain implementation issues of GST at the state level.

Usha Mathur provided able secretarial assistance. I hope this book will help in the understanding of the process of implementation and outcome of a complex tax reform called GST in an even more complex country called India.

New Delhi
May 2019

PINAKI CHAKRABORTY

One

Goods and Services Tax

Rationale and Key Issues

The introduction of the goods and services tax (GST) is expected to abolish the fragmented tax regime, help develop a common market in India, eliminate cascading of taxes, and help increase gross domestic product (GDP) growth by promoting trade, business and investment.

GST was launched on 1 July 2017 amid much fanfare. Dubbed as the single-largest reform since independence, it is expected to propel India into a unified market by bringing a uniform system of indirect taxation across the country and removing a plethora of state-specific levies. A host of other countries around the world have implemented GST (often called value-added tax or VAT)[1] in some form or the other, throughout the latter half of the twentieth century. France was the first to introduce it in 1950 as the French production tax (Bird and Gendron 2001). Currently, some form of VAT exists in 160 countries.[2] But different countries have devised their own unique VAT structures over the years, moulding it according to their local conditions and compulsions. In most cases, political economy compulsions determine what kind of VAT fits a country. There is no one-size-fits-all solution. Therefore, it is crucial to realise that the VAT environment is highly dynamic—more countries continue to adopt it, and those that already have it continue to reform its design and implementation (International Tax Dialogue 2005). It also implies that the social, political and economic context of tax reform cannot be ignored.

India is a highly diverse country, with its own unique characteristics. It is a Union of states with 29 state governments, seven centrally administered Union territories and the Union government. Before the introduction of GST, our Constitution allowed the Union to collect taxes on production, while states were allowed to tax consumption of goods.[3] It was only in 1994 that the Union government started taxing services separately. Prior to that, services were not taxed in India. The Union government started levying service tax as per the 'residuary power' in the Constitution. This had created a distortion in consumption taxation in the country. While the power to tax consumption of goods remained with the states, the power to tax services became a Union government responsibility. This had also created a fragmented taxation system for consumption by two different levels of government, leading to various inefficiencies, distortions and complexities in administering the consumption tax.

With the introduction of GST, the separate tax powers of the Union and the states have been merged and both levels of government are now allowed to tax from a common tax base that comprises both goods and services. Application of GST follows the destination principle, which implies that taxes are imposed only on final consumption and not on production. Also, remaining true to the core idea of VAT, taxes paid on inputs are refunded as input tax credits. This eliminates cascading of taxes, resulting in economic efficiency gain. The original plan was to introduce GST from 1 April 2010, but the process got delayed by more than seven years. This delay is a reflection of the fact that the political economy of tax reforms is complex in a federal country like India.

The idea of a comprehensive GST was first mooted in the Union budget of 2007–08 by the then finance minister P. Chidambaram. The deadline for its implementation was set as 1 April 2010 in the budget speech itself. Although this policy announcement brought the Union and the states together to decide on the contours of GST, they could not arrive at a consensus for the appropriate design of GST. There were many conflicting issues that required resolution through negotiations between all stakeholders. Three critical issues were the rate of tax, the number of rates for GST and the issue of compensation to the states by the Union government in case of revenue loss. Also, the richer producing states in India were apprehensive about their potential revenue loss due to the introduction of GST as it worked on the destination principle. It also meant a direct loss of revenue from central sales tax (CST), as GST required the elimination of CST. We discuss these issues in greater detail in the book. The discussion that follows explains the rationale behind the introduction of GST.

Rationale behind GST

GST is a comprehensive VAT on goods and services. Many countries in the world have introduced VAT to replace pre-existing turnover taxes or import tariffs in an attempt to make their domestic economies more competitive internationally, especially in the context of increasingly open economies. A comprehensive VAT on goods and services is a broad-based consumption tax and is supposed to provide a neutral, stable and buoyant source of revenue. The nature of business and the structure of industry and trade are expected to become more efficient and cost-effective post-GST. However, when the GST base is not comprehensive, the revenue performance of the tax is seriously undermined. For instance, in a regime that allows for input tax credit, if a number of segments of the economy are exempt from taxation, this increases the scope for tax fraud, as all the people who buy goods do not need invoices.

Countries in the South Asian region have witnessed considerable resistance to introducing a comprehensive GST. Most have VAT only on goods, leaving the fast-growing services outside the GST net, and many do not extend the scope of the tax beyond the manufacturing stage. Too many exemptions remain a concern in these countries' VAT design. In Pakistan, for instance, VAT, which is just called sales tax or general sales tax, is a tax administered by the federal as well as provincial governments. However, the federal government has taxation powers only in the matter of goods; thus, taxation of services is decided at the province level. Pakistan has multiple tax rates, starting with 17 per cent for goods, and 13 per cent, 15 per cent and 16 per cent for services, with at least eight reduced rates. The problem of reduced rates is faced in Bangladesh as well, where, apart from a standard rate of 15 per cent, numerous reduced rates apply, which range from 1.5 per cent to 10 per cent. In Sri Lanka, VAT was introduced in 2002, which incidentally replaced the goods and services tax that existed before. Here, VAT offers minimum exemptions and there is a single VAT rate of 15 per cent, which was increased from 11 per cent in November 2016. In Maldives, GST was introduced in 2011 at the standard rate of 6 per cent. The tax applies to the supply of both goods and services. Moreover, given the high dependence of the Maldivian economy on tourism, the government also has a separate 12 per cent tourism GST. In Nepal, the value-added tax co-exists with excise duties. Although the exports are zero-rated, consistent with the destination principle of VAT, there are many exemptions that narrow down the tax base. Nepal has a standard rate of 13 per cent, which applies to both goods and services. The Bhutan tax regime does not have a VAT or VAT-like regime yet, and it taxes most goods via excise duty (that is currently levied only on alcoholic beverages at 30 per cent, 60 per cent and 75 per cent), sales tax (ranging from 0–100 per cent) and a green tax (ranging from 5–30 per cent) in cases of import of motor vehicles, petrol and diesel. In Afghanistan, VAT has been in discussion for a very long time and has seen several rounds of discussions and negotiations, supported and facilitated by the International Monetary Fund (IMF). Recently, an IMF report (2018) noted that Afghanistan should prepare for the introduction of VAT by January 2021 by replacing the current business receipts tax.

India used to have a VAT on goods up to the manufacturing stage, a separate services tax at the Centre, and VAT on goods up to the retail stage by individual states. The transition to GST has changed this permanently and is expected to bring benefits to the economy. Central and state taxes subsumed under GST are listed in Table 1.1.

This list shows the taxes that have ceased to exist under the new tax regime. However, petroleum products, alcohol for

Table 1.1: Various Union and State Taxes Subsumed under GST

Union taxes subsumed under GST	*State taxes subsumed under GST*
Central excise duty	State VATs
Additional excise duty	Central sales tax (levied by the Centre and collected by the states)
Additional and special additional duty on customs	Luxury tax
Service tax	Octroi and entry tax
Central cess	Entertainment tax (other than the tax levied by the local bodies)
Surcharges, so far as they relate to the supply of goods and services	Taxes on advertisement
	Purchase tax
	Taxes on lotteries, betting and gambling
	State surcharges and cesses, so far as they relate to supply of goods and services

Source: Department of Economic Affairs, Ministry of Finance.

human consumption, the real estate sector and electricity duty are kept out of the purview of GST. In other words, while most indirect taxes have been subsumed under GST, a large part of it still remains outside. Incomplete coverage of goods and services is indeed an issue that India needs to resolve as it moves further on the path of reform of indirect taxes to get the full benefits of GST as well as for a comprehensive coverage. However, the present structure of GST is a vast improvement from the earlier indirect tax regime. The GST Council, the constitutional body responsible for the design and architecture of GST, has started discussing the possibility of including petroleum products under GST to limit cascading and to increase the coverage.

Why is GST Desirable?

A tax is distortionary by its very nature.[4] However, given its indispensability, a tax structure should be designed in such a way that it minimises distortionary effects. Barro and Sala-i-Martin (1992) highlight the importance of a well-designed tax system by showing that such a system can minimise efficiency losses imposed by taxes and can also raise the GDP growth rate. Besley and Persson (2011, 2013, 2014a, 2014b) identify taxation, especially broad-based taxation, as an important determinant (along with political and institutional factors) of a state's capacity to provide crucial public services and function efficiently. Adhikari (2015) finds a positive and economically significant relation between adopting VAT and the real GDP per worker on a panel of 167 countries. However, a lot is contingent upon the level of development, tax evasion and the size of the informal economy. This implies that the efficiency gains arising from VAT may be different for a developed and a developing country.

A well-designed VAT (or GST) has many advantages over other forms of taxes due to which it is preferred the world over. One of the major arguments for VAT is that it brings efficiency to economic activities. A VAT taxes all the stages of production but refunds the taxes paid on inputs used in production. This serves two purposes:

one, it removes the cascading of taxes since taxes are only levied on the value added at a particular stage to avoid taxing the tax; and two, it reduces incentives for vertical integration. Taxes that are levied on input costs plus taxes promote firms to integrate all the stages of production under a single entity. This is done in order to minimise the incidence of taxes, as the supply of goods within a firm is not taxed. But such a practice seriously limits economic efficiency gains arising due to specialisation. Thus, as a form of an indirect tax regime, VAT is more efficient than its alternatives. For India, the move to subsume a number of indirect taxes under the VAT-able GST should bring considerable efficiency gains. Substantial welfare and economic advantages should also accrue post the introduction of a significantly simpler tax.

A VAT also reduces tax evasion due to its self-enforcing design. It is relatively easy to evade taxes in a single-stage sales tax regime by just underreporting sales, but it is quite difficult in a VAT regime. VAT induces businesses to demand invoices from their suppliers to obtain credits for the taxes paid on their purchases. A failure to obtain such invoices disqualifies the businesses from securing tax refunds on the inputs used. Moreover, multi-stage taxation ensures that full tax is collected at the next stages of production, even if the tax had been evaded at an earlier stage. To completely evade VAT, all the firms in the production and distribution chain will have to work in collusion to hide their sales, an activity requiring considerable effort and costs, thus disincentivising evasion. Furthermore, in light of the audit trail that VAT transactions create, Bird and Gendron (2007: 31) note that 'since the two sides of the transaction are (for inter-business trade) in principle recorded in two sets of books, the task of the administration in detecting evasion should be easier with VAT'.

The Goods and Services Tax Network (GSTN) in India (discussed later) is expected to work on this principle. It is expected to make auditing quick and easy with information regarding purchases and sales made available by the businesses themselves through various returns. However, it is always difficult to replicate a theory in real life, and evasion can still be persistent. Although paper trails exist for all the stages of production since they are required for the purposes of tax refund, final consumers do not have much incentive to request sales receipts, making tax evasion a possibility. Such a phenomenon has been observed in Chile. When 'deterrence letters' were sent to randomly selected firms in Chile, those firms increased the reporting of their final sales, but not of intermediate sales, indicating a possible underreporting of final sales previously (Pomeranz 2015). Furthermore, a high tax rate regime also promotes tax fraud. High tax rates have universally been accepted as a powerful motivation for evasion. Artavanis (2015) reported an increase of 11.8 per cent in the average sales to input ratio following a 10 per cent reduction in VAT for non-alcoholic sales in Greece, implying a significant uncovering of unreported sales. This makes it clear that a strong tax administration, a simple framework and reasonable tax rates are all keys to ensure a proper implementation of VAT and keep a check on evasion.

A VAT should be based on the 'broad-based low rate' approach, i.e., it should be applicable to all consumption in the economy with minimal or no exemptions. This broadening of the tax base gives policymakers the freedom to set a lower tax rate in order to earn tax revenue similar to that of the earlier tax regime, while still improving on the simplicity of the tax system. Taxing everything at a lower rate is preferred over taxing a few things at a higher rate. Thus, VAT ensures stable revenue inflows, provided that too many exemptions and the consequent narrowing down of the base are strictly avoided. The revenue through VAT is further aided by the efficiency and the simplicity that a broad-based tax brings to the system. Thus, frequently resorting to increasing the VAT rate to collect more revenue goes against the spirit of VAT. Emphasis should be laid on broadening the tax base and reducing the exemptions under VAT as much as possible. The significance of a broad base can be understood through the VAT revenue ratio, a measure used by the Organisation for Economic Co-operation and Development (OECD) to assess member countries' VAT performance. This ratio expresses the VAT revenue that is actually collected by a country as a proportion of the VAT revenue that would be collected if the standard VAT rate were applied to all consumption without any exemption. Figure 1.1 plots the VAT revenue ratios of various OECD countries.

Figure 1.1: VAT Revenue Ratios of OECD Countries

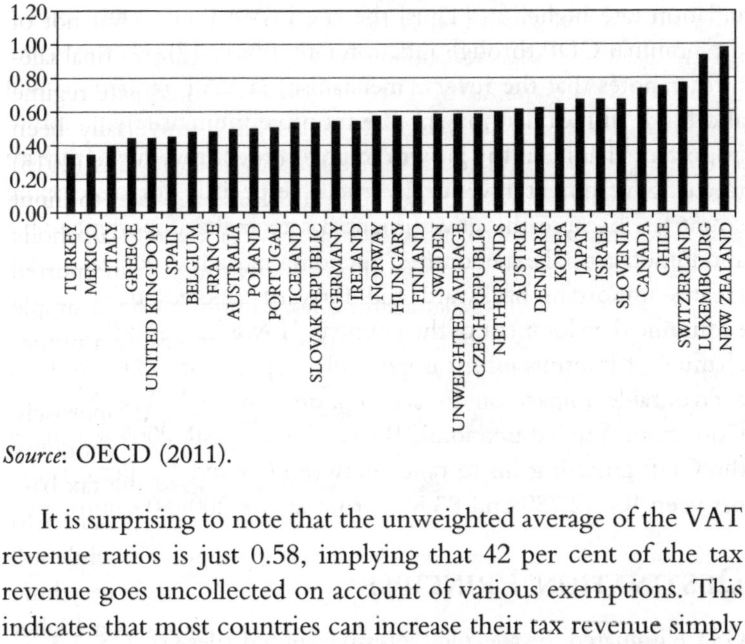

Source: OECD (2011).

It is surprising to note that the unweighted average of the VAT revenue ratios is just 0.58, implying that 42 per cent of the tax revenue goes uncollected on account of various exemptions. This indicates that most countries can increase their tax revenue simply by bringing more items under the tax net, rather than increasing levies on already taxed commodities. A similar economic burden is caused by rampant evasion and non-compliance. The European Union Commission in a 2009 study estimated the gap in the VAT collection, caused by fraud, avoidance and insolvencies, to be close to 106.7 billion euros (Jeffery 2011).

Introducing VAT in a country can have substantial impact on its economy, since it effectively discards the previous regime and anoints in its place a new one. A change in the VAT rate is also a significant event since it affects the production and consumption of almost all goods and services. Thus, VAT will always have a significant bearing on the economy. But since the economic growth of a country is determined by a host of factors, the exact channel of such an impact is country-specific and mostly non-general. Two of the most important channels for the transmission of VAT's impact are inflation and government revenue. Miki (2011), in his study of a panel of 14 developed countries, finds a positive relation between VAT and inflation. He proposes that '[a] rise in VAT makes the inflation rate higher.... [Thus] the rise in VAT rate will increase the nominal GDP through inflation rate' (ibid.: 17). However, he further notes that the reverse mechanism (a VAT reduction) will also hold, an idea that may not be intuitive immediately. Another important channel is the growth in government revenues. Increase in the government revenue is crucial, especially for developing countries, because the government has to make important social and infrastructural expenditures. Spending in such structural sectors creates important backward and forward linkages that aid the economic development of the country. However, regardless of the channel of transmission, it is generally hoped that GST will have a favourable impact on India's economy as well. The National Council of Applied Economic Research (NCAER 2009) estimates the GDP growth gains to range between 0.9 and 1.7 per cent, or between Rs 42,789 and 83,899 crore at the 2008–09 numbers.

Destination Principle

GST eliminated the age-old regressive central sales tax (CST). CST was a regressive tax levied at the point of production, resulting in significant tax exportation from the richer producing states to the poorer consuming states, contributing to fiscal inequality in the country. This is the reason why some of the richer producing states were not happy with the abolition of CST and were initially opposed to the idea of GST. Some of them are still not happy with GST. It is expected that the expansion of the base due to the destination principle of taxation at the point of consumption and additional taxation of services would result in significant revenue gain to states after the input tax credit adjustment and loss of CST revenue. At one point, the draft Constitutional Amendment Bill for GST introduced a provision of 1 per cent CST, which was eliminated when the bill was finally passed by both the Houses of the Parliament. Had it not been the case, the benefits of GST would have been eroded substantially with the continuation of origin-based taxation.

GST and the Constitution of India

The introduction of GST also required a constitutional amendment (122nd Constitutional Amendment) to enable the Union government to tax consumption of goods and states to tax consumption of services. Post the constitutional amendment, both the Central and the state tax bases have merged. Henceforth, both levels of government will collect taxes from this common base, encompassing goods as well as services. The constitutional amendment enabled the creation of the GST Council. The council's chairperson is the Union finance minister. States have their finance ministers as members of the council. Since the creation of the council in November 2016, it has met 25 times. On an average, meetings of the council happened almost on a fortnightly basis, bringing clarity to the design, rate structure and mechanisms for compensation under GST. This also shows that the Indian federal system has transformed itself in a way where both the Centre and states have learnt to trust each other and give up their exclusive taxation rights with respect to a particular tax base for a better tax system and the benefit of the economy. The expectation is that this common tax base creation would result in the abolition of the fragmented tax regime, the development of a common market, the elimination of cascading of taxes, and increase in the growth of GDP by promoting trade, business and investment.

Is this really happening? What has been the experience of GST implementation so far? What are the measures taken to simplify the tax structure post-GST? Have trade, business and industry really found it easy to do business and comply with the GST laws? Where does consumer interest stand in this overall structure of GST reform? Has the tax compliance burden really declined? These are some of the issues that this book intends to address. At this stage, an important caveat needs to be mentioned. I had started writing this book when GST was just six months into its implementation. Today, it is well over a year old. Answers to some of the questions raised in this book, therefore, are indicative, based on my assessments, and are not definitive conclusions.

Has GST Compromised Federalism?

This book also discusses the issue of federalism in the context of GST. It is certainly true that the right to taxation is intimately linked with the right to decide on the rate of taxation. Post-GST, individual state governments will no longer decide on the rate structure of GST in their respective states. In this way, for the sake of tax harmony, fiscal autonomy is compromised. This is true for the Central government as well. The Centre also cannot change anything without the approval of the majority of the states in the GST Council. But if we examine the big picture, fiscal policy, especially pursuing an independent tax policy, has in a way become ineffective post the global integration of the Indian economy. To give an example, to attract global investment, India really cannot have a corporate income tax rate that is way above the rates in other emerging market economies that are trying to attract the same investment. A similar undertone exists in this scenario as well, i.e., a process of harmonisation of tax rates across the country through a process of negotiation in the GST Council between the Union and state governments. In the former case, it is the market that forces a country to align rates to a particular reference. In the latter case, the same is happening through a process of negotiations among the stakeholders. The larger question, thus, is: Is rate harmonisation alone sufficient to attract trade and investment? Probably not. We need to have a harmonisation of processes as well. If business and trade have to face different kinds of complexities in complying with the tax in different states, rate harmonisation would become ineffective.

Finally, the post-GST fiscal architecture is an outcome of the 101st Constitutional Amendment. It is too late to reopen this issue. Autonomy of all levels of government, including that of the

Union government, has been tied to the GST Council on matters of indirect taxation. It is the responsibility of the council to work in a manner that preserves and strengthens the fiscal autonomy of all levels of government. The Union government would have to take the lead in this regard. Whatever happens, this process is irreversible. The broad objective of the book in this context is to contribute to the debate on GST with an objective to provide policy insights that can improve the design and structure of GST for the benefit of the economy and the consumer.

Notes

1. Many scholars differentiate between the two on the basis that VAT does not include services. However, this may not be true for many countries. GST and VAT have been used interchangeably in this book.
2. Ministry of Finance, Malaysia, http://www.treasury.gov.my/pdf/gst/list_of_countries.pdf (accessed 21 June 2018).
3. The Constituent Assembly discussed whether prohibition should be mandated by the Constitution, but it could not come to a decision. Finally, it agreed to make it a state subject, which led to states getting the power to tax the consumption of alcohol.
4. A tax artificially increases the price of a commodity. The extra money collected in the form of tax revenue goes to the government from the consumers—an internal transfer within the economic system, which does not make the system any richer or poorer as a whole. However, since the price has artificially gone up, some transactions do not take place, i.e., consumers forgo some of their consumption, thus reducing economic activity in the system.

Two

History of Indirect Tax Reforms and the Evolution of GST

For every rupee that the governments in India earn, almost 72 paise comes from indirect taxes. Due to so much importance attached to indirect taxes, governments over the years have made multiple attempts to reform these taxes. The most important reform in this list is the introduction of GST.

Dependence of governments on trade taxes as a major source of revenue is a common feature in most developing countries. In 2015–16, India derived around 65 per cent of its tax revenue from indirect tax sources. Usually, due to the intrinsically regressive nature of indirect taxes, heavy dependence of governments on them as a major revenue source is seen as a problem. Indirect tax regime in India, prior to the introduction of value-added tax (VAT) in 2005 and GST in 2017, suffered from a number of problems. As highlighted in *Reform of Domestic Trade Taxes in India: Issues and Options* (1994), a report by the National Institute of Public Finance and Policy (NIPFP), the indirect tax regime in India suffered from the following deficiencies:

1. Heavy reliance on taxes at the manufacturer/first-seller level.
2. Exclusion of services from the tax base for a very long time.
3. Taxation of inputs and capital goods.
4. High and multiple rates with too many exemptions.
5. Complex tax laws and disharmony between tax laws among states.

Some of the above-mentioned problems are summarised below to understand the rationale behind the transition from an archaic indirect tax system to VAT at the state level in 2005 and to GST in 2017. The discussion on the problems with the old tax regime in this section is heavily drawn from the NIPFP report (1994).

Taxing the Manufacturer: The term 'manufacturing' is not easy to define. Besides regular manufacturing, there are many processes that can be termed as 'marginal manufacturing'. Thus, attempts to tax such activities have often resulted in disputes and litigations. Court rulings sometimes made matters more complex rather than resolving them. A judicial ruling is a case in point. The court held that while the assembling of a cycle from its parts in CKD (completely knocked down—a fully disassembled item) shall not qualify as a manufacturing activity, the assembling of fishing rods out of imported components will. A further issue in manufacturing has been with regard to the calculation of assessable value for tax purposes. In determining the assessable value, problems related to adjustments for 'legitimate' trade margins and treatment of transactions between related entities cropped up frequently.

Exclusion of Services: This, for a very long time, was a significant lacuna in the indirect taxation system. Before 1994, services were not taxed in India. This inadvertently led to a production and consumption bias against goods and in favour of services. This was also not in consonance with the economic realities of the country. Thus, while introducing service tax, the then finance minister Manmohan Singh observed in his budget speech of 1994, 'this sector [services] accounts for 40% of our GDP.... [Thus] there is no sound reason for exempting services from taxation when goods are taxed and many countries treat goods and services alike for taxation purposes.'

Taxation of Inputs and Capital Goods: Faced with a narrow base and mounting pressure for revenue, governments also taxed inputs used in the production process. Such taxation led to cascading of taxes and proved to be inefficient. This cascading was especially large for some commodities (e.g., fertilisers), for which the gap between the effective incidence of sales tax and excise duty combined and the nominal tax rate was around 12 per cent (Aggarwal 1995). In the longer run, more serious consequences like vertical integration and disincentive to specialisation can be directly attributed to the taxation of inputs. A tax on capital inputs is particularly harmful. Such a tax discourages investment activities in the economy, thus directly affecting employment and growth. Efforts were made to rationalise the system through the introduction of VAT on manufacturing. However, the impact was minimal due to the multiplicity of rates and numerous exemptions.

High and Multiple Rates: The governments resorted to raising the tax rates in the face of a narrow base and the need for more revenue resources. Frequently, additional levies were also imposed over and above the taxes when it became difficult to raise the tax rates any further. This made the system arbitrary and unpredictable. Unreasonably high rates also increased the incentive for evasion and the pressure for exemptions and concessions. This manifested in the form of multiple rates, often based on 'hair-splitting' classifications and distinctions between sectors and goods, and leading to serious inefficiency and unnecessary disputes regarding such classification. By 1994, over 42,000 excise cases were pending before the appellate tribunal and high courts. High rates also aggravated the distortionary effects of indirect taxation.

Importance of Indirect Taxes in Indian Public Finance

Despite all the aforementioned inefficiencies, indirect tax continued to be the most important source of revenue in India,[1] and its importance has only increased over the years. India's indirect tax to GDP ratio in 1950–51 was 3.81 per cent (Table 2.1), but this ratio has since increased substantially. Currently, it stands at 11.95 per cent of GDP. From Table 2.1, it emerges that throughout the history of independent India, indirect tax has been the dominant

Table 2.1: Combined Revenue Receipts of the Centre, States and Union Territories as a Percentage of GDP (at Current Market Prices)

Taxes	*1950–51*	*1960–61*	*1970–71*	*1980–81*	*1990–91*	*2000–01*	*2010–11**	*2013–14*	*2014–15*	*2015–16 (RE)*	*2016–17 (BE)*
Direct Taxes	*2.22*	*2.24*	*2.12*	*2.18*	*2.09*	*3.30*	*5.79*	*5.78*	*5.64*	*5.55*	*5.65*
Corporation Tax	0.38	0.61	0.78	0.88	0.91	1.64	3.84	3.51	3.44	3.29	3.24
Taxes on Income	1.29	0.94	0.99	1.01	0.92	1.46	1.79	2.12	2.07	2.12	2.27
Land Revenue	0.50	0.54	0.25	0.10	0.10	0.06	0.10	0.08	0.07	0.08	0.09
Others	0.06	0.53	0.71	0.20	0.16	0.13	0.07	0.07	0.06	0.05	0.05
Indirect Taxes	*3.81*	*5.29*	*7.86*	*11.08*	*12.87*	*10.73*	*10.55*	*10.95*	*10.72*	*11.78*	*11.95*
Customs	1.51	0.95	1.10	2.28	3.52	2.18	1.74	1.53	1.51	1.52	1.51
Union Excise Duties	0.65	2.32	3.69	4.34	4.18	3.15	1.77	1.51	1.52	2.06	2.08
Service Tax	–	–	–	–	–	0.12	0.91	1.38	1.35	1.53	1.51
State Excise Duties	0.48	0.31	0.42	0.59	0.85	0.73	0.79	0.76	0.76	0.82	0.83
Stamp Duties and Registration Fees	0.27	0.26	0.28	0.29	0.36	0.43	0.70	0.72	0.70	0.73	0.74
Sales Tax	0.56	0.91	1.65	2.68	3.11	3.35	3.77	4.23	4.06	4.26	4.40
Others	0.34	0.53	0.71	0.89	0.85	0.77	0.86	0.82	0.84	0.86	0.88
Tax Revenue	*6.03*	*7.53*	*9.98*	*13.26*	*14.96*	*14.02*	*16.34*	*16.73*	*16.36*	*17.32*	*17.60*

Note: * Data before 2011–12 is based on the 2004–05 series. For 2011–12 onwards, it is based on the 2011–12 series.
Source: Author's calculations, based on Indian Public Finance Statistics (various editions).

revenue source for governments. Figure 2.1 presents the percentage share of the indirect tax to GDP ratio in the total tax to GDP ratio. This ratio was 63.21 per cent in 1950–51, but it increased to as high as 86.02 per cent in 1990–91. Thereafter, the share started declining. Such high dependence on indirect taxes was a result of the low personal income tax base. This forced governments to depend more on taxing transactions. This is also reflected in the excessive revenue derived from excise duties and sales tax. Out of the 12.87 per cent indirect to GDP ratio in 1990–91, 7.29 per cent was derived from these two heads. After 1991, the share of direct taxes in the total tax revenue started increasing, although indirect taxes continued to be, and still are, the major revenue source.

A closer look at the numbers also reveals another interesting undercurrent—the decreasing relative importance of indirect taxes in the overall government tax revenues until recently. Table 2.2 presents the absolute and percentage changes in the indirect tax

Figure 2.1: Shares of Direct and Indirect Tax to GDP Ratios in the Total Tax to GDP Ratios

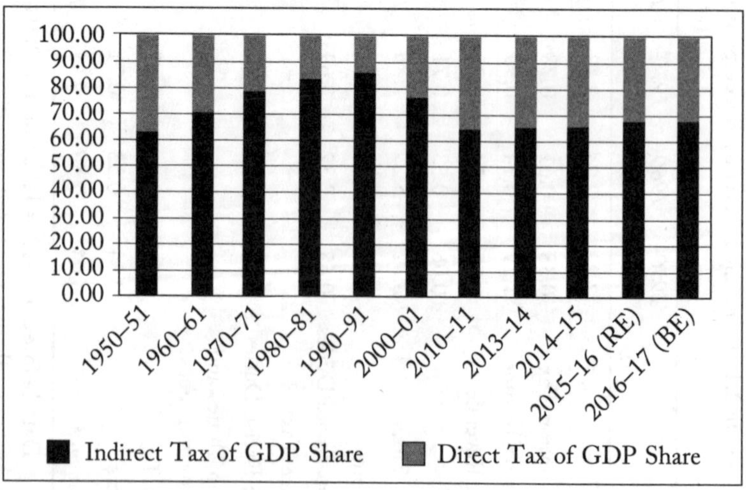

Source: Author's calculations, based on Indian Public Finance Statistics (various editions).

Table 2.2: Absolute and Percentage Changes in the Tax to GDP Ratios for Direct, Indirect and Total Tax Revenues for the Government

	Change from 1950–51 to 2016–17		*Change from 1990–91 to 2016–17*		*Change from 1950–51 to 1990–91*		*Change from 2010–11 to 2016–17*	
	Absolute (I)	*Percentage (II)*	*Absolute (III)*	*Percentage (IV)*	*Absolute (V)*	*Percentage (VI)*	*Absolute (VII)*	*Percentage (VIII)*
Direct	3.43	155%	3.56	170%	–0.13	–06%	–0.14	–2%
Indirect	8.14	214%	–0.93	–07%	9.06	238%	1.40	13%
Total	11.57	192%	2.63	20%	8.94	148%	1.26	8%

Source: Author's calculations, based on Indian Public Finance Statistics (various editions).

to GDP and direct tax to GDP ratios for the years 1950–51 to 1990–91, 1990–91 to 2016–17, 2010–11 to 2016–17, and 1950–51 to 2016–17. From 1950 till 2016, the indirect tax to GDP ratio increased by 214 per cent, while the direct tax to GDP ratio increased by 155 per cent (columns I and II). However, the indirect tax to GDP ratio constituted around 70 per cent of the total tax to GDP ratio increase. But the importance of indirect taxes was even greater in the pre-liberalisation period of 1950–51 to 1990–91 (columns V and VI). In this period, while the direct tax to GDP ratio reduced by a marginal 6 per cent, the indirect tax to GDP ratio increased by a whopping 238 per cent, which contributed to all the increment in the total tax to GDP ratio in the 1950–91 period (Table 2.3). But this reliance on indirect taxes has been on the decline since the liberalisation of the economy. With rising incomes and rationalisation of direct taxes, the governments have tried to make taxation more progressive by reducing the reliance on indirect taxes, while increasing the revenue from direct taxes. The direct tax to GDP ratio increased by 170 per cent in the 1990–91 to 2016–17 period, even though the indirect tax to GDP ratio reduced marginally. What is more, the increase in the direct tax to GDP ratio made up all the increase in the total tax to GDP ratio in the post-liberalisation period. In the period between 2010–11 and 2016–17, the reliance on indirect taxes increased marginally.

Table 2.3: Share of Direct and Indirect Tax to GDP Ratios in Changes in the Total Tax to GDP Ratios

	Share of Direct Taxes in the Total Tax to GDP Ratio Increase	*Share of Indirect Taxes in the Total Tax to GDP Ratio Increase*
From 1950–51 to 2016–17	30%	70%
From 1950–51 to 1990–91	–1%	101%
From 1990–91 to 2016–17	135%	–35%
From 2010–11 to 2016–17	–11%	111%

Source: Author's calculations, based on Indian Public Finance Statistics (various editions).

Although the significance of indirect taxes has waned in recent times, its importance as a major revenue source for the governments remains unchallenged. For every rupee that the governments in India earn, almost 72 paise comes from indirect taxes. Due to so much importance attached to indirect taxes, governments over the years have made multiple attempts to reform these taxes. Some of these significant attempts are discussed in the next section.

Attempts to Reform the System

The system of indirect taxation in India has witnessed substantial reforms over the years, especially in the past few decades. In the post-independence era and up to the 1970s, the reform activities for taxation were mostly limited to direct taxes. As for indirect taxes, only some piecemeal attempts were made to reform its various aspects. The principal objective of these attempts was to enhance revenue productivity by widening the tax base and increasing tax rates. Unsurprisingly, the indirect tax system remained archaic. Multiple forms of excise duties and sales taxes created a cascading effect and acted as an impediment to voluntary compliance as well as for attaining the objective of a rational indirect tax system[2] (Vaidya and Kangasabapathy 2013).

The Indirect Taxation Enquiry Committee, formed in 1976 under L. K. Jha,[3] was the first serious attempt towards reforming indirect taxes.[4] The committee submitted its report in 1977 and observed that indirect tax in India, rather than reflecting the economic needs of the country, evolved mostly as a reaction to the problems that arose over time. The system had transformed into a mess of high and multiple rates, causing vicious cascading. The committee, as an example, cited the case of anti-diabetic drugs. The nominal excise and sales rates imposed on an important anti-diabetic drug were 2 per cent and 4 per cent, respectively. However, the cumulative levy added up to a whopping 27 per cent.

The committee's report was widely considered the most exhaustive study on indirect taxation at that time. It identified the distortionary effects of indirect taxes in the allocation of resources and recommended a move towards taxation of final products and a modified form of VAT.[5] Drawing upon the recommendations of the committee, in 1986, India undertook a major reform initiative and introduced the modified value-added tax (MODVAT). This was further converted into a central value-added tax (CENVAT). Again, in 1991, the Tax Reforms Committee under the chairmanship of Raja J. Chelliah recommended a gradual conversion of excise duties from MODVAT to VAT. The transition to VAT from the pre-existing sales tax regime[6] was a major reform in indirect tax as well as in the overall tax administration of India.

The Expert Group on Taxation of Services, under the chairmanship of M. Govinda Rao, was constituted in 2001 and was tasked with recommending reform measures in service taxation. Services comprised almost 50 per cent of GDP, but almost 95 per cent of the sector was out of the tax net. Thus, it was considered necessary to tax the services sector. The expert group gave several recommendations, some of which are listed in Box 2.1. In addition, the reformed service tax was to be administered electronically. Although the recommendations were not fully implemented, it is clear that the expert group envisaged a service tax system much

Box 2.1: The Recommendations of the Expert Group on Taxation of Services

- Comprehensively cover the services sector under the service tax net, with minimal exemptions and, possibly, a negative list.
- A threshold of 10 lakh for tax payment.
- Exemptions of certain services that are either developmental in nature or cater to the lower strata of society.
- The ultimate integration of service tax with CENVAT.
- Provision of input tax credit.
- Electronic administration of tax to cut down inconveniences and facilitate voluntary compliance.
- Sharing the power to tax services with states.

Source: Ministry of Finance, Government of India (2001).

on the lines of the current GST. It may not be wrong to suggest that the origin of the current GST regime can be traced to the expert group's report.

As already noted, service tax was introduced in 1994 and had a very small coverage to begin with. However, with time, its coverage was increased, as was the rate. Over time, it became an important component in the government's indirect revenue portfolio. The revenue collected from service tax increased from Rs 407 crore in 1994–95 to Rs 2,31,000 crore in 2016–17 (Figure 2.2). While the service tax revenue growth remained volatile, the steady increase in revenue could be attributed to the continuous expansion of the base of service tax by increasing the coverage of service taxation. In the budget of 2012–13, the concept of a negative list was introduced for service tax. This was a list of services exempted from service tax, i.e., every service not part of the list was taxable automatically. This was a significant departure from the earlier practice of maintaining a positive list of taxable services. It not only broadened the base of service taxation by

Figure 2.2: Revenue Collection and Growth of Service Taxes

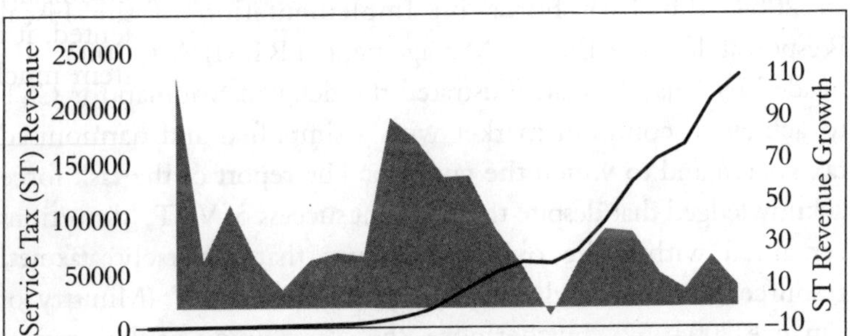

Source: Author's calculations, based on Indian Public Finance Statistics 2016–17.

increasing coverage, but also brought considerable simplification in the implementation of the tax.[7]

Post the introduction of service tax, the Union government decided to introduce VAT in 1995 towards abolishing multiple points of taxation on goods and rationalising the overall tax burden. It further envisaged the objectives to benefit common people, traders, industrialists and also the government by providing a simpler and more transparent tax system. Most states introduced a VAT in 2005, which was levied only on intra-state trade with the provision for input tax credit (ITC). Interstate transactions continued to be governed by the CST. Thus, ITC was not available for interstate purchases (Vaidya and Kangasabapathy 2013). In other words, apart from the exclusion of services, India had only experienced a partial VAT regime until 2017 due to various reasons, including the exclusion of interstate sale from VAT.

In July 2002, the Task Force on Indirect Taxes under the chairmanship of Vijay Kelkar suggested measures for the simplification and rationalisation of indirect taxes (Ministry of Finance and Company Affairs 2002). Its recommendations laid down the foundation of the Goods and Services Tax (GST). In 2004, the Task Force on Implementation of the Fiscal Responsibility and Budget Management (FRBM) Act, 2003, also headed by Vijay Kelkar, illustrated the detailed roadmap for GST to achieve a common market with a simplified and harmonised tax system and to widen the tax base. The report of the task force acknowledged that despite the apparent success of VAT, 'distortions remained within the overall structure that adversely affected resource allocation and efficiency of administration' (Ministry of Finance 2004: 52). Furthermore, the contribution of the services sector in the GDP had increased substantially over the years. Thus, the exclusion of the services sector from the tax base restricted the revenue productivity of the tax system. Although the service tax and Union excise duties were individually comprehensive, they did not prove to be enough to reap the revenue productivity of the services sector. The FRBM report further pointed out that 'independent taxation of goods and services under different legislations created the same kind of problems as selective taxation of services' (ibid.: 55). Additionally, the blurred line between goods and services ultimately led to more disputes, the resolution of which, through circulars and courts, proved to be extremely burdensome. Although all disputes must necessarily end in the Supreme Court, even after a decision by the Supreme Court, it was immensely difficult to give effect to the principles enunciated by the highest court.

With the advent of digital technology, the line between goods and services is blurring further. As noted in the FRBM report,

> Goods and services have become indistinguishable and can be subjected simultaneously to a tax that is applicable only to goods and at the same time under a law that is intended to primarily tax services. Besides, there is a strong interdependence of goods and services in the production and distribution activities in the economy. (ibid.)

Apart from the factors related to revenue and litigation, integration of taxes on goods and services is also necessary to reduce administrative and compliance costs and complexities.

From the preceding discussion, two things emerge clearly: first, a fully integrated service tax with the existing CENVAT on goods, i.e., a modern VAT-type levy on all goods and services is a more efficient form of indirect taxation. Second, GST is not entirely a new concept—it is a comprehensive VAT on the supply of goods as well as services, which addresses the shortcomings of the earlier VAT system that only taxed goods.

Potential Benefits of GST

There are many benefits of GST, which are well-evident from various global experiences. The following are some of its benefits:

- GST brings about a drastic change in the indirect tax system by redistributing the burden of taxation equitably between manufacturing and services. Simultaneously, it simplifies and broadens the tax base by including more services under a single tax and also by minimising various exemptions. This in turn raises the overall revenue productivity of the indirect tax system.

- It reduces the number of taxes at the central and state level, thus fostering a common market across the country with reduced compliance costs.
- It reduces transaction costs of taxpayers through simplified tax compliance, and leads to increased tax collections due to a wider tax base and better compliance.
- GST reduces distortions by completely switching to the destination principle. By reducing market distortions, GST has the potential to spur economic growth. It has been estimated by the NCAER (2009) that a comprehensive GST across goods and services will increase GDP growth by about 0.9–1.7 per cent.
- The effective tax rate generally declines as GST removes the cascading effect of taxes. It reduces the costs of manufactured goods and services and increases the competitiveness of Indian goods and services in the international market.
- It promotes exports, making the domestic market more competitive. The NCAER (2009) study on the impact of GST on foreign trade indicates that the terms of trade move in favour of agriculture vis-à-vis manufactured goods within a range of 1.8 to 3.8 per cent. The study also found that the rate of growth of exports would be significantly higher than that of imports post-GST. GST is also expected to promote employment.
- The Union government's 'White Paper on Black Money' (Ministry of Finance 2012) envisages that GST will foster the growth of the legitimate economy and will prevent the generation of black money.
- In recent years, it has also been argued that GST will result in increased formalisation of the economy.

Despite these benefits of GST and even after the announcement by former finance minister P. Chidambaram in the budget speech of 2007–08 for a shift to the GST regime from 1 April 2010, the implementation of GST only happened on 1 July 2017.

History of GST Negotiation

Taking into account the recommendations of various committees and experts, the discussions with trade and industry, and the consultations with the Government of India, the Empowered Committee of State Finance Ministers released the 'First Discussion Paper on Goods and Services Tax in India' in November 2009 (Box 2.2). The discussion paper provided a design for a common tax system on the sale of goods and provision of services, keeping in mind the state and Union tax structure. It proposed a dual levy

Box 2.2: First Discussion Paper on Goods and Services Tax in India: Key Highlights

The then finance minister P. Chidambaram announced, in his 2007–08 budget speech, the government's intention to introduce GST in the country from 1 April 2010. This led to the formation of an Empowered Committee of State Finance Ministers that, in consultation with the Central government, was tasked to chalk out the structure of GST and the probable roadmap for its implementation. This empowered committee presented to the country its first discussion paper on 19 November 2009. The paper was meant to facilitate discussions regarding GST with various stakeholders from industry, trade and agriculture, and the general public at large.

Building on the development of VAT in the country, which was first introduced in the form of MODVAT in 1986, the committee contended that the movement from VAT to a more comprehensive GST was a logical transition. To support this argument, it pointed out several flaws in the contemporary VAT regime prevalent in the country at that time. Some of these are as follows:

1. Non-inclusion of several Central indirect taxes and indirect taxes at the state level in the CENVAT and state VATs, respectively. This caused a non-comprehensive input tax credit (ITC) coverage.
2. The VAT-ability of taxes was only limited to the manufacturing processes. Distribution trades were excluded from it.

(*Contd*)

(*Box 2.2 contd*)

3. The CENVAT load in goods' value remained when the state VATs were charged, leading to cascading on account of CENVAT.
4. Despite the importance of services in most manufacturing processes, service tax was not VAT-able. This again led to a loss of ITC.

Keeping these issues in mind, some of the design features recommended by the committee were as follows:

1. GST to have two levies: at the Centre, called the Central GST, and the state level, called the state GST. Further, an integrated goods and service tax (IGST) to be levied for interstate supplies. It also recommended uniformity in GST across states and at the Union level as far as practicable.
2. Both goods and services to be taxable.
3. CGST and SGST to be paid separately in the accounts of the Centre and states, respectively.
4. ITC of CGST to be set off against tax liabilities of CGST only, and similarly for SGST. Cross-utilisation of ITC allowed only in case of IGST.
5. Both the Centre and the states to have concurrent jurisdiction over all the GST taxpayers.
6. A single registration threshold for manufacturers as well as service providers.
7. Exclusion of alcoholic beverages and petroleum products from GST, and inclusion of tobacco products with ITC.
8. Payment of compensation to the states by the Union for any loss in revenue for the initial five years after the implementation of GST.

In addition, the committee identified the need for various constitutional amendments and the framing of various legislations and rules to enable the implementation of GST. Apart from some variations, the final GST design today in India relies heavily on the initial structure suggested by the empowered committee in 2009.

Source: The Empowered Committee of State Finance Ministers (2009).

of GST (concurrently by the Centre and the states) to broaden the tax base, get rid of tax cascading and move to a common tax base, and also subsume various Central and state levies on goods and services into a Central goods and services tax (CGST) and state goods and services tax (SGST), respectively.

Soon the Task Force on Goods and Services Tax constituted under the Thirteenth Finance Commission also came out with its report with recommendations for 'a flawless' GST in India.[8] The design of GST suggested in the report purportedly seeks to eliminate tax distortions, impose a tax on consumption and thereby make different stages of production and distribution a mere tax pass-through, and, most importantly, create a single common market for all. The design of the GST model recommended by the task force discussed, in a fairly comprehensive manner, aspects required to draft a complete GST law. The standout aspect (something that had been a subject of considerable debate) was the proposal for a single revenue neutral rate (RNR) of 12 per cent (CGST at 5 per cent and SGST at 7 per cent). This was a dramatically lower rate than what had been anticipated so far and the final rate of GST discussed in the Empowered Committee of State Finance Ministers. A study by Rao and Chakraborty (2010) made alternative estimates of RNRs for the Empowered Committee of State Finance Ministers. The rates proposed by Rao and Chakraborty (ibid.), based on the data of 2007–08, are reproduced in Table 2.4. As is evident, in a two-rate GST structure, for states alone, the proposed rates were in the range of 10–12 per cent, with wide interstate differences.

Another significant discussion that the task force engaged in was around who governs GST. From past experience on the implementation of VAT, the inherent autonomy of states with regard to the power to tax had led to a wide divergence in tax rates across states. A sensible GST therefore meant complete harmonisation of the tax base, tax rates, tax procedures and compliances. To achieve this objective, the task force recommended the conversion of the empowered committee into a permanent constitutional body known as the Council of Finance Ministers, comprising the Union finance minister and all state finance ministers. The task force also suggested that the council should approve any modification in the final design of GST. This was a very significant proposal. The GST Council that has finally

Table 2.4: Revenue Neutral Rates (RNRs) with and without a Comprehensive Base

	RNRs		*RNR with a Comprehensive Base*	
	Single Rate	*Two Rates*	*Single Rate*	*Two Rates*
Andhra Pradesh	9.3	11.69	9.96	12.4
Bihar	6.8	7.72	8.46	9.35
Chhattisgarh	12	15.47	9.39	10.51
Goa	9.07	11.36	3.9	3.8
Gujarat	11.82	15.26	12.22	15.51
Haryana	10.72	13.71	10.21	12.21
Kerala	8.78	10.22	8.82	9.96
Karnataka	9.67	12.18	11.05	13.84
Madhya Pradesh	9.65	11.95	10.53	12.54
Maharashtra	9.84	12.19	12.12	15.74
Odisha	10.49	13.22	9.68	11.12
Punjab	9.62	11.95	8.46	9.69
Rajasthan	9.63	12.09	9.05	10.69
Tamil Nadu	9.25	11.53	10.85	13.68
Uttar Pradesh	9.05	11.11	9.99	12.3
West Bengal	8.35	9.85	9.46	11.27
All States	9.69	12.05	10.3	12.52

Source: Rao and Chakraborty (2010).

evolved is indeed a constitutional body responsible for all aspects of the implementation of GST. The task force report provided a workable model with proper guidelines for every aspect of law. It indeed provided a sensible design of the model GST and recommendations on various issues that remained unaddressed in the first discussion paper. Among its major recommendations were the suggestions for a phased inclusion of the real estate sector into GST and the elimination of stamp duty. As is evident from Table 2.5, the actual design of GST is vastly different from the GST structure proposed by the empowered committee and the task force.

Table 2.5: Design of GST: Key Proposals and the Actual Design

Key GST Aspects	*Empowered Committee Proposal*	*Finance Commission Proposal*	*Design Adopted by the GST Council*
Rate of GST	Multiple rate structure for goods and single rate for services (rates not disclosed).	Recommends a single rate of 5 per cent for CGST and 7 per cent for SGST, with power to states to levy surcharge in the event of crisis for one year, subject to conditions.	Five rates for various categories of goods: 0 per cent, 5 per cent, 12 per cent, 18 per cent and 28 per cent. A special 3 per cent rate on precious metals. All rates to be divided equally between the Union and states.
Classification of Goods and Services	Distinguishes between goods and services by proposing differential treatment and thresholds for each.	Recommends uniform treatment for both goods and services to avoid classification issues.	Adopted uniform treatment of both goods and services. Draws distinction between nil-rated, zero-rated, exempt and non-GST goods.
Purchase Tax	Subsuming of purchase tax under debate.	Purchase tax proposed to be subsumed.	Purchase tax subsumed.
Sin Goods (emission fuels, tobacco and alcohol)	Tobacco to be covered under GST, whereas other sin goods to be kept outside GST.	All sin goods should be subjected to a dual levy of GST (creditable) and state excise duty (non-creditable).	Sin goods like *pan masala* and other tobacco products placed under the highest slab of 28 per cent rate. Alcohol for human consumption kept out of GST's purview, and it will continue to attract the old VAT and excise duty.

(*Contd*)

(*Table 2.5 contd*)

Key GST Aspects	*Empowered Committee Proposal*	*Finance Commission Proposal*	*Design Adopted by the GST Council*
Exempt Supplies	Would list exempt goods; possibly the current list under VAT legislations to be adopted.	Discourages exemption. Restricts it to specified public services of the government: unprocessed food under the public distribution system; health and education services.	Exempted supplies include nil-rated supplies, non-GST supplies and any other goods notified by the government as exempt. Among others, alcohol for human consumption, and petrol and petroleum products are significant exemptions from GST.
Special Economic Zone (SEZ)	Supplies to processing zones in SEZ proposed to be zero rated.	Recommended no exemption for the developers of or units in SEZs.	Supplies to an SEZ developer/unit are zero-rated. Supplies from an SEZ developer/unit attract IGST at 18 per cent.
Treatment of Interstate Transactions	Proposed IGST model to deal with interstate transactions.	Recommends a modified bank model to deal with interstate transactions; does not support the adoption of the IGST model.	Interstate transactions attract IGST at 18 per cent.
Treatment of Consignment or Branch Transfers	The discussion paper is silent on this aspect.	Equates consignment or branch transfers to interstate sales for taxability purposes.	Interstate branch transfers treated as interstate sales with the input tax credit (ITC) available. Consignment transfers treated as transactions between two separate parties, and thus taxable under GST with the benefit of ITC.

(*Contd*)

(*Table 2.5 contd*)

Key GST Aspects	*Empowered Committee Proposal*	*Finance Commission Proposal*	*Design Adopted by the GST Council*
Threshold Limits	Different thresholds for goods (i.e., Rs 15 million for CGST and Rs 1 million for SGST) and for services (Rs 1 million for SGST and limit to be decided for CGST).	Uniform threshold of Rs 1 million for goods and services recommended under both the levies.	Uniform threshold limit for both goods and services of Rs 20 lakh (with Rs 10 lakh for north-eastern and hilly states).
Tax payments	CGST and SGST to be paid separately; SGST to be paid to the credit of respective states.	Single monthly payment for CGST and SGST to be made electronically (vide return cum *challan*); even SGST pertaining to various states to be included in single monthly payment. Further, clarity provided with respect to the periodicity of tax payments and returns.	A normal taxpayer is typically required to file three monthly returns, along with an annual return, electronically. Businesses do not need to file separate returns for CGST, IGST and SGST.
Tax Administration	Proposed that legislation would be drafted for tax administration, dispute resolution and advance ruling.	Recommends that the Central Board of Excise and Customs (CBEC) would administer CGST and the state tax administrations should be responsible for SGST, such that a tax payer should interface only with one authority for both CGST and SGST (based on specific criteria).	The Central government administers CGST, IGST and Union territory GST (UTGST) through the Central Board of Indirect Taxes and Customs (CBIC) (earlier the CBEC). SGST is governed by the respective state governments.

Source: Empowered Committee of State Finance Ministers (2009); Thirteenth Finance Commission (2009).

Compensation to States in GST Regime

A theoretical justification of the rationale behind the Central government compensating GST-induced revenue loss could be twofold: (i) the positive externality argument, and (ii) the balancing of unequal loss across states due to differences in their tax structure. The positive externality argument emanates from the fact that the introduction of GST will eliminate the inequality that current internal trade taxation gives rise to and also help reduce the economic distortions and inefficiency in economic decision-making and resource allocation. As the positive externality of the introduction of VAT would benefit the economy as a whole, the Union government, which has a better command over resources, should compensate the resultant revenue loss. The second argument for compensation arises from the fact that the tax structure of states is different due to differences in the manufacturing base across states—correspondingly, the resultant revenue loss will be different, which needs to be compensated by the Union so that horizontal inequality is not accentuated further.

The primary apprehension about revenue loss arises on the full and comprehensive input tax rebate that has to be provided to input purchase, loss on account of interstate sales or CST loss due to its elimination and the full input tax rebate thereon, input tax credit on branch transfers, and consignment sales and exports and transitional loss. At the same time, there will be revenue gains arising out of taxing value addition at every stage of production and that of services up to the retail stage by the states. Ultimately, the estimation of revenue loss needs to be adjusted against the revenue gains that GST would possibly generate through higher economic growth due to non-distortionary taxation. In short, the basic objective of the tax system is to make it neutral to trade and business decision, externally and internally. Revenue loss apprehension held back GST implementation for a long time.

GST Implementation

Following the presidential assent to the GST Bill, the Union government created the GST Council. Since then, the Council has met regularly to arrive at an acceptable GST structure. The GST Council has recommendatory powers which are stated in Article 279A (4) of the Indian Constitution. As per the Council's website,[9]

> it will make recommendations to the Union and the States on important issues related to GST, like the goods and services that may be subjected or exempted from GST, model GST Laws, principles that govern Place of Supply, threshold limits, GST rates including the floor rates with bands, special rates for raising additional resources during natural calamities/disasters, special provisions for certain States, etc.

In other words, the entire architecture of GST is decided by the GST Council. Given this, one had thought that the road ahead would not be easy and negotiations in the GST Council stormy. However, the way the GST Council has worked in the past few months is commendable. Every decision in the GST Council so far has been based on consensus.

Constitutional Mandate and Functioning of the GST Council

The ultimate benefit of GST would depend on the design of the tax, which is dependent on the various provisions of the GST Bill. Of course, a purist would aspire for a 'flawless GST'. But in reality, GST has never been flawless anywhere in the world. What we need is a broad base, a distortion minimising tax system for our indirect taxes for goods and services. Three major constraints imposed by the constitutional amendment are partial coverage of the base of GST, voting mechanism to arrive at decisions in the council and absence of clarity on dispute settlement among the stakeholders. The coverage is not comprehensive. For revenue consideration, petroleum products are kept out of GST. Since a large part of the petroleum products are intermediate inputs, and such use will not be eligible for input tax credit, there will be cascading of taxes post-GST. In relation to the harmonisation of tax, as per the bill, the GST Council is required to formulate a model GST law to recommend to the Union and states. This is a step towards harmonisation of the tax system across the country. Although tax harmonisation is often perceived as rate harmonisation, particularly by business and industry, it needs to be emphasised that despite a single rate, if trade and industry have to face very different tax laws across states, it would increase the transaction cost of business. Hence, a model GST law recommended by the GST Council to the Union and states is a welcome move. Of course, it is not obligatory for the Union and the states to adopt the model GST law. But if the model is treated as the foundation and then customised in the specific context of a state, keeping the broad principles of the model law in place, it would help to evolve a harmonised tax system. In the bill, the GST Council has been given special provisions for the special category states. The rationale behind introducing GST was to have a simplified tax system, minimise distortion and maximise economic efficiency gain, and this requires minimum exemptions, broadening of the base and imposition of a low rate. It is hoped that special provisions do not become the norm and complicate the tax system. It is necessary that these special provisions are used judiciously.

Why the Dispute Settlement Mechanism Needs Flexibility

Since GST is based on a common tax base, both levels of government have surrendered their exclusive taxation power with respect to a particular base. This is indeed a reflection of the element of trust and maturity the Indian federal fiscal system has moved to over the years, and it should certainly provide a sense of satisfaction to all. This is also a reflection of greater economic integration in the country and of the aspiration for a common market. However, the degree of fiscal power that has been surrendered by both the Union and the states is asymmetric. The combined tax revenue of the Union and states subsumed under GST is roughly Rs 8,000 billion. In this combined kitty, Central revenue accounts for roughly 46 per cent and state revenues account for 54 per cent. As a percentage of the Union's tax revenue, the share of taxes to be collected under GST works out to be 40.17 per cent. For the states, this is 70 per cent. In other words, what the states are surrendering as their exclusive taxation right is much more than the Union in this bargain. Naturally states are far more apprehensive in this negotiation with the Union. Any Union–state deliberation on the subject of GST should be sensitive to this reality of tax reform. One of the sticky points of GST negotiations arising from this particular issue was that of compensation to states by the Union government in case of revenue loss after the introduction of GST.

For the comfort of the states, GST compensation is a part of the constitutional amendments. This should certainly allay the fear of states as compensation has now become a legal right and uncertainties related to the actual flow of compensation in case of revenue loss from the Union to the states is settled. If implemented properly, given the experience of VAT, it is unlikely that the states would have a major revenue loss. In fact, if economic growth pushes up, a broad-based GST with a reasonable rate should result in revenue gain rather than loss of revenue for both the Union and the states.

The Most Contentious Issue: The Rate of GST

Fixing the rate of GST remains a big question. The GST Council decides the rates of GST. If we consider the VAT rate in the European Union, standard rates vary from 18 per cent to 27 per cent (Table 2.6). It appears that there is an argument to keeping the standard rate of GST as 'not exceeding 18 per cent'. However, there is a strong merit in the argument that one cannot have an excessively

Table 2.6: VAT Rates in the European Union

Member States	*Super Reduced Rate*	*Reduced Rate*	*Standard Rate*
Belgium	–	6/12	21
Bulgaria	–	9	20
Czech Republic	–	10/15	21
Denmark	–		25
Germany	–	7	19
Estonia	–	9	20
Greece	–	6/13	23
Spain	4	10	21
France	2,1	5,5/10	20
Croatia	–	5/13	25
Ireland	4,8	9/13,5	23
Italy	4	10	22
Cyprus	–	5/9	19
Latvia	–	12	21
Lithuania	–	5/9	21
Luxembourg	3	8	17
Hungary	–	5/18	27
Malta	–	5/7	18
The Netherlands	–	6	21
Austria	–	10	20
Poland	–	5/8	23
Portugal	–	6/13	23
Romania	–	5/9	24
Slovenia	–	9,5	22
Slovakia	–	10	20
Finland	–	10/14	24
Sweden	–	6/12	25
United Kingdom	–	5	20

Source: http://ec.europa.eu/taxation_customs/resources/documents/taxation/vat/how_vat_works/rates/vat_rates_en.pdf (accessed 20 September 2018).

high rate for GST. It is important to arrive at a reasonable rate that is acceptable to both the Union and state governments. There is always scope for revising the rates, depending on the revenue collection. The experience of VAT is a case in point. VAT was started with a standard rate of 12.5 per cent in 2005. Over the years, it has been increased to 14.5 per cent. Such options should be available with the GST Council to ensure that revenues do not decline and for reasons such as changing macroeconomic circumstances.

Voting Rights and Functioning of the GST Council

The new bill—Constitution (122nd Amendment) (GST) Bill, 2014—allows for a voting process instead of a consensus, with the Central government having a weight of one-third of the total votes cast and state governments (taken together) having a weight of two-thirds of the total votes cast. As per entry 9 of the Article, 'Every decision of the Goods and Services Tax Council shall be taken at a meeting, by a majority of not less than three fourths of the weighted votes of the members present and voting.'

With the passing of the bill, individual states as well as all states together lost fiscal autonomy as far as changes in the GST design is concerned. Since any change would require three-fourths of the total votes and the Union government accounts for one-third of the vote share, without the Union government's approval, changes cannot be carried out. Surrendering fiscal autonomy fully for a tax that provided more than two-thirds of the state revenues—a share that is likely to go up post-GST—needs careful consideration. This issue is critically important for the states, more than for the Union government.

GST: Fiscal Autonomy versus Tax Disharmony

As mentioned earlier, the combined tax revenue of the Union and states subsumed under GST is roughly Rs 8,000 billion. In this combined kitty, Central revenue accounts for roughly 46 per cent and state revenues account for 54 per cent. As a percentage of the Union's tax revenue, the share of taxes collected under GST works out to be 40.17 per cent. Although the rate structure is decided, appropriate apportionment of this rate between the Union and state governments is critical so as to ensure the revenue autonomy of each level of government. On the distribution of RNR between the Union and states, the report of the Committee on RNR, headed by the Chief Economic Advisor, noted that the allocation of rate

> must reflect the revenue requirements of the Centre and States so that revenues are protected. For example, a standard rate of 17% would lead to rates at the Centre and States of say 8 percent and 9 percent, respectively because that is roughly the ratio of GST revenues that would have to be generated by the Union and States assuming that the 2013–14 data on which these estimates are calculated remain valid. (Ministry of Finance 2015: 30)

According to the committee, 'it would be preferable to keep all other rates identical between the Centre and states to minimise distortions and facilitate compliance' (ibid.).

If we consider the combined indirect tax to GDP ratio for the year 2013–14, it was 11.39 per cent, of which the Union government's indirect tax to GDP ratio was 4.65 per cent. In other words, states on an average were collecting around 60 per cent of the total indirect taxes in the country and that was roughly the entire own tax revenue of the states. States do not have any major direct tax sources. Since the predominant source of this indirect tax revenue is VAT on goods, it is expected that post-GST, this revenue will be protected.

Since we have a dual GST in an overlapping tax base, substantial fiscal autonomy has been surrendered by both levels of government. A unified GST has implications for not only trade and business but also the basic federal structure, particularly the fiscal structure and the resultant vertical and horizontal imbalances. In this context, protecting state-level fiscal autonomy is critical. One of the key aspects of fiscal autonomy is the ability to fix the rate.

In a multi-level fiscal system, fiscal autonomy is not just about the independent financial power of sub-national governments. It is also critical for accountability. In this context, it is worth mentioning what Amaresh Bagchi observed when the idea of a national GST was first announced by P. Chidambaram in the 2006 budget: 'Revenues that flow from the Union cannot be regarded as something that the recipient governments are politically responsible for raising. Politicians and bureaucrats may find it convenient to avoid the onus of raising the monies they like to spend, but that way lies the road to fiscal irresponsibility' (Bagchi 2006: 1315). Going a step forward, it may not be wrong to argue that the GST Council should apportion the rate structure in such a way that it reduces the existing vertical fiscal imbalance and provides appropriate fiscal space for greater accountability of all levels of government.

The constitutional amendment itself has imposed constraints on implementing a broad-based GST by keeping petroleum products out of the purview of GST. This has rendered the base partial and allowed the continuance of cascading of taxes. As per the amendment, these goods shall not be subject to the levy of GST till a date notified on the recommendation of the GST Council. As argued earlier, it is important that a specific date for inclusion of these items under GST is decided by the GST Council at the earliest and acted upon towards universal application of coverage of the tax base for an efficient outcome.

NOTES

1. Revenue from indirect taxes is still the major source of tax revenue, although various tax reforms were undertaken during the 1990s. The major argument put forth for heavy reliance on indirect taxes is that the majority of India's population is poor, and thus widening the base of direct taxes has inherent limitations (Kumar 2015). The majority of the population in India falls technically outside the ambit of direct taxes. According to a report released by the Ministry of Finance, the estimated number of taxpayers for the financial year 2011–12 stands

at just 3.24 crore. This means that less than three people in 100 pay taxes. Out of these 3.25 crore people, 89 per cent pay taxes in the tax slab of 0–5 lakh rupees, while on the other end of the spectrum, only 1.3 per cent of all tax payers have an income of about 20 lakh, which is quite unacceptable. See https://www.financialexpress.com/india-news/letters-to-the-editor-24/16209/ (accessed 4 September 2018).

2. The consumption tax (indirect tax) system in India is complicated and multilayered, with levies both at the federal and state levels. Taxes on goods are levied by the Centre at the manufacturing level through the central value-added tax (CENVAT), on services through the Finance Act and on sale of goods via the Central Sales Tax Act. States levy tax on the sale of goods independently, under their own laws. Although some degree of uniformity had been arrived at after the introduction of VAT, differences do persist.

   The complex state-wise indirect tax structures have meant that manufacturers base their inventory and distribution decisions on tax avoidance instead of operational efficiency. Accordingly, most manufacturers maintain warehouses in different states to evidence movement of goods from one warehouse to another to save on the central sales tax (CST). Also, quite a few entities set up warehouses in locations like Puducherry or Daman, often impractical from a distribution point of view, as the CST rate at such locations were previously lower than the rates prevalent in other states.
3. He was then the Governor of Jammu and Kashmir.
4. However, its recommendations were not implemented for over a decade, and then too, only partially.
5. The Jha Committee actually recommended the introduction of manufacturers' value-added tax (ManVAT) in the union excise duties.
6. Under the General Sales Tax Act, which had been in force since 1957.
7. Finance Minister Pranab Mukherjee, in his budget speech of 2012–13, observed, 'Movement towards the negative list will result in reducing nearly 290 definitions and descriptions in the Act to 54, and the exemptions from the existing 88 to 10.... In terms of number of pages, the law will be shorter by nearly 40 per cent' (https://www.indiabudget.gov.in/budget2012-2013/ub2012-13/bs/bs.pdf [accessed 19 February 2019]).

8. The 'flawless' GST was expected to subsume all the major state-level taxes, use a single rate, allow for only essential exemptions and eliminate all barriers to trade.
9. http://gstcouncil.gov.in/gst-council (accessed 19 February 2019).

Three

Issues under Transition

On 1 July 2017, GST was introduced with an unusually large number of rates. Multiple rates and a very high rate of 28 per cent appeared to have had an adverse announcement effect.

Numerous debates, both inside and outside Parliament, various committees examining the fine aspects of its structure, lengthy negotiations by the Centre with the state governments and concerted efforts to explain it to the general public—the amount of work that has gone into making the goods and services tax (GST) a reality is immense. However, there are still a few areas of concern, some related to structure and design—for example, the multi-rate structure that reduces the benefits from GST—while others are related to the impact of GST on various fundamentals of Centre–state relations, like its effect on the fiscal autonomy of states. This chapter discusses some such important challenges and impacts of GST.

Since GST subsumed the tax spaces of both the Union and the states, which are specified in the Union, state and concurrent lists,[1] it was necessary that the Constitution of India be amended suitably before the GST could be implemented. The amendment to the Constitution was, however, not easy. The Government of India, in consultation with the states, introduced the Constitution (115th Amendment) Bill, 2011 (GST Bill) in the Lok Sabha on 22 March 2011 to facilitate the introduction of GST. This bill was the fourth draft ever since the discussions on the implementation of GST began in 2007. The earlier three drafts proposed by the finance ministry were rejected by the states on the grounds that the drafts threatened to take away their fiscal autonomy. The bill was referred to the Standing Committee on Finance (Chairman, Shri Yashwant Sinha) on 29 March 2011. The Standing Committee on Finance submitted its report on the bill in August 2013. However, with the dissolution of the 15th Lok Sabha, the pending bill lapsed.

A new government (National Democratic Alliance [NDA-2]) assumed power on 26 May 2014 and introduced the Constitution (122nd Amendment) Bill, 2014 in the Lok Sabha on 19 December 2014 to facilitate the introduction of the GST regime in India, with the expectation that the new tax would be implemented from 1 April 2016. Following protracted negotiations with the states and debates in Parliament, Lok Sabha passed the bill on 6 May 2015. In the Rajya Sabha, the bill was referred to a Select Committee on 14 May 2015, which submitted its report on the bill on 22 July 2015. Rajya Sabha passed the bill on 3 August 2016, and Lok Sabha passed the amended bill on 8 August 2016. The bill, after ratification by the states, received assent from President Pranab Mukherjee on 8 September 2016 and was notified in *The Gazette of India* on the same date. Except five states, viz., Jammu and Kashmir, Karnataka, Kerala, Manipur and West Bengal, all other states ratified the bill. The key features of the Constitution Amendment Bill passed by both Houses of Parliament are reproduced in Box 3.1.

While the basic features of the bill ultimately passed by the Parliament remained more or less the same, some of the issues that delayed the process of introduction of GST may be worth highlighting here. The insertion of Article 246A provides concurrent power to the Union and state governments to make laws on the taxation of both goods and services. However, the Union government may levy and collect GST on supplies in the course of interstate trade and commerce. The taxes collected from interstate trade and commerce would be divided between the Union and states in a manner laid down by the Parliament by law, on the recommendation of the GST Council. As per the bill, the GST Council would make recommendations on the model GST law, principles of levy, apportionment of integrated

Box 3.1: Main Provisions of the GST Bill

- Insertion of a new Article (246A) to confer simultaneous power to Union and state legislatures to legislate on GST.
- A new Article (279A) is proposed for the creation of a GST Council, which will be a joint forum of the Centre and the states. This council would function under the chairmanship of the Union finance minister and will have ministers in charge of finance/taxation or a minister nominated by each of the states and Union Territories with legislatures as members. The council will make recommendations to the Union and the states on important issues like tax rates, exemptions, threshold limits and dispute resolution modalities.
- To do away with the concept of 'declared goods of special importance' under the Constitution.

The proposed GST has been designed keeping in mind the federal structure enshrined in the Constitution and will have the following important features:

- Central taxes like central excise duty, additional excise duties, service tax, additional customs duty or countervailing duty (CVD) and special additional duty (SAD) of customs will be subsumed under GST.
- At the state level, taxes like value-added tax (VAT) or sales tax, central sales tax, entertainment tax, octroi and entry tax, purchase tax and luxury tax would be subsumed under GST.
- All goods and services, except alcoholic liquor for human consumption, will be brought under the purview of GST. Petroleum and petroleum products have also been constitutionally brought under GST. However, it has also been provided that petroleum and petroleum products shall not be subject to the levy of GST till notified at a future date on the recommendation of the GST Council. The present taxes levied by the states and the Centre on petroleum and petroleum products—sales tax/VAT, central sales tax (CST) and excise duty—will continue to be levied in the interim period.
- Both the Centre and the states will simultaneously levy GST across the value chain. The Centre would levy and collect the central goods and services tax (CGST), while the states would levy and collect the state goods and services tax (SGST) on all transactions within their respective states.
- The Centre would levy and collect the integrated goods and services tax (IGST) on all interstate supply of goods and services. There will be seamless flow of input tax credit (ITC) from one state to another. Proceeds of IGST will be apportioned among the states.
- GST is a destination-based tax. All SGST on the final product will ordinarily accrue to the consuming state.

Source: The Constitution (122nd Amendment) Bill, 2014.

goods and services tax (IGST) and the principles that govern the place of supply. The GST Council is required to recommend to the Union and the states the design of GST, including the taxes, cess and surcharges levied by the Union, and various taxes levied by states and local bodies that may be subsumed under GST. The council would also recommend the goods and services that may be subjected to or exempted from GST; the threshold limit of turnover below which goods and services may be exempted from GST; the rates, including floor rates, with bands of GST; special rate(s) for mobilisation of additional resources in times of any natural calamity or disaster; and special provisions with respect to various special category states. The GST Council shall recommend the date on which GST will be levied on petroleum crude, high speed diesel, motor spirit (commonly known as petrol), natural gas and aviation turbine fuel. In other words, the GST Council has to develop the entire architecture of GST involving the Union, states and the Union Territories, along with the legislature.

FEDERALISM AND THE BASIC STRUCTURE OF THE CONSTITUTION

Federalism has been held to be one of the basic features of the Constitution. The Constitution provides three lists in the Seventh Schedule: the 'Union List' (exclusive domain of the Parliament), the 'State List' (domain of state legislatures) and the 'Concurrent List' (both). On Concurrent List subjects, when there is an inconsistency between laws made by Parliament and laws made by state legislatures, the former shall prevail. This structure gives supremacy to the legislative power of the Parliament in all cases except the State List. The GST Bill gives both the Union and the states equal power to make laws related to GST (without the Parliament's law overriding the state law). The question is: Does this change in the nature of legislative powers exercised by the Union and the states affect the basic structure of the Constitution? On this issue, the Task Force on GST opined that a 'dual levy imposed concurrently by the Union and the States, but independently' will promote cooperative federalism (Thirteenth Finance Commission 2009: 5).

Potential Conflict between Legislative, Judicial and Executive Bodies

Under the Constitution, the power to impose taxes is vested with the Parliament and state legislatures. The GST Council, however, is responsible for the design and structure of GST. It is also responsible for tax harmonisation across states and between the Union and states under the GST regime. The bill has created a structure through which an executive body (the GST Council) recommends and decides the tax rates, and all the stakeholders implement the GST Council's decisions. This has impinged on the right of legislatures to determine tax rates. The Supreme Court has ruled that courts cannot advise the executive or adjudicate on the wisdom, correctness or suitability of a policy. They may only consider its legality. Also, under the present system, there is no mechanism to enforce the GST Council's decision. If a state deviates from the council's decision, there is no direct mechanism available to the GST Council to make the state follow its decision. All decisions of the GST Council so far have been by 'consensus' of all members.

Major Departure from the Earlier GST Bill

The key areas of divergence of the Constitution (122nd Amendment) Bill, 2014 passed in the Lok Sabha from the Constitution (115th Amendment) Bill, 2011 are: (a) coverage, (b) functioning of the GST Council, and (c) design of GST, other than the aspect of coverage. A comparison of the two bills will provide insights into what has changed and its implications for the GST design.

Coverage

The 122nd Amendment Bill defines GST as any tax levied on the supply of goods or services, except taxes on the supply of alcoholic liquor for human consumption. However, the 115th Amendment Bill excluded taxes on supply of (i) petroleum-crude, (ii) high speed diesel, (iii) motor spirit (petrol), (iv) natural gas, (v) aviation turbine fuel, and (vi) alcoholic liquor for human consumption from the purview of GST. In this sense, the amended bill increases the coverage of goods and services under GST, and it is certainly an improvement over the earlier provision. However, for petroleum and petroleum products, the 122nd Amendment Bill has provided that these goods shall not be subject to the levy of GST till a date notified on the recommendation of the GST Council.

It needs to be emphasised that since a large part of petroleum and petroleum products are important intermediate inputs, it is absolutely necessary to bring them under the GST ambit sooner rather than later to eliminate cascading and its associated inefficient economic cost. Even in a GST regime, these could be taxed at a higher rate if revenues have to be protected. It is well-known that petroleum and petroleum products and alcohol together contribute around 40–45 per cent of the VAT/sales tax revenues of states. The share of excise duty collection from petroleum and petroleum products is substantial for the Union government as well. It appears that revenue consideration alone is holding back the inclusion of these items in GST. It is necessary for the bill to specify a specific date for the inclusion of these items under GST, especially when the economic efficiency benefit from inclusion is much more than the direct short-run revenue impact on the Union and state governments. Both the Thirteenth Finance Commission and department of revenue had recommended that petroleum products be included within the purview of the GST. Petroleum products are inputs for many products and services, and exempting them will lead to tax cascading. The Thirteenth Finance Commission had recommended bringing a dual levy system for petroleum products, tobacco and alcoholic liquor. This would entail subjecting such products to GST, while allowing states and the Union to levy an additional excise. Under the bill, only tobacco products are subject to such a treatment (the Union may levy excise).

Expanded Purview of the GST Council in the New Bill

While both the bills required the GST Council to make recommendations on the design of GST, the additional functions in the 122nd Amendment include the following: (i) model GST laws, principles of levy, apportionment of IGST and the principles that govern the place of supply; (ii) any special rate for a specified period to raise additional resources during any natural calamity or disaster; (iii) special provision with respect to Assam, Arunachal Pradesh, Jammu and Kashmir, Manipur, Meghalaya, Mizoram, Nagaland, Sikkim, Tripura, Himachal Pradesh and Uttarakhand.

The GST Council formulating a model GST law that will be recommended to the Union and states is a step towards harmonisation of the tax system across the country.

Interstate GST

Both bills provide for the Centre to levy and collect GST on supplies in the course of interstate trade or commerce. However, the difference arises in terms of the principles of apportionment and the levy of additional tax.

Regarding the sharing of proceeds, the 122nd Amendment provides for the GST Council to make recommendations for the apportionment of IGST as well as formulate principles governing the place of supply. The bill states,

> Goods and services tax on supplies in the course of inter-State trade or commerce shall be levied and collected by the Government of India and such tax shall be apportioned between the Union and the States in the manner as may be provided by Parliament by law on the recommendations of the Goods and Services Tax Council.

The earlier bill stated that the tax collected would be divided in a manner prescribed by Parliament by law. Additionally, under both the bills, Parliament may pass a law (if it chooses) to determine when the supply of goods or services (or both) occurs in interstate trade.

GST Compensation

While the earlier bill did not provide for compensation—though there was always an assurance of compensation to the states—the 122nd Amendment Bill states that Parliament may, by law, on the GST Council's recommendations, provide for compensation to states for revenue losses arising out of the implementation of GST, for a period of up to five years. This should provide comfort to the states. The new bill deletes the provision that permits states to tax entry of goods into a local area for use or sale only to the extent levied by a panchayat or municipality (while the earlier version allowed this). This is certainly an improvement as it will increase the coverage and also eliminate tax-induced fragmentation of the market. This deletion would help develop a common market post-GST.

Design Issues

After prolonged debates and discussions among stakeholders for several years, the broad framework of GST is now a dual GST in line with the proposal made in the first discussion paper of the Empowered Committee of State Finance Ministers (2009). So, in the GST model, both the Central and state GST components are levied on the same base, i.e., it is a dual tax system, and barring a few exceptions, all goods and services are brought into the GST base. More importantly, the distinction between goods and services for the purpose of the tax is eliminated and a common legislation is applicable to both. However, within the proposed dual GST structure, a number of issues are yet to be resolved. These issues are discussed subsequently and in the chapters to follow.

Determination of Base and a Revenue Neutral Rate

Prior to the introduction of GST, the determination of the tax base and the corresponding revenue neutral rate (RNR) was the most contentious issue. The Task Force on GST of the

Thirteenth Finance Commission had come up with its estimates of RNR, which were incredibly low. It posed serious doubts about the validity of the estimate itself and the consequent revenue risk (Rao and Chakraborty 2010), where the primary concern of all state governments was protection as well as enhancement of existing revenue streams. The task force's estimate of RNR at 11–12 per cent (5 per cent for the Union and 6–7 per cent for the states) was possible only if the GST base was comprehensive, with a minimum number of exempted goods and services in the list. With regard to RNR, many have held the view that the rate cannot be too high, yet must be high enough to address the concerns of states regarding revenue neutrality. Also, there were people favouring a single rate as it would ensure low compliance costs, obviate classification disputes and ensure a uniformity of approach amongst all players.

An argument that gained ground was that if the governments did not increase the tax base or reduce the number of items that attract a lower tax rate, the potential RNR in GST could be quite high and politically unpalatable. Despite prolonged discussions, both the Union and the states were unable to arrive at an acceptable RNR for GST. Although GST is already in force, its success would depend critically on the rate of taxation. There is an urgent need to have a very realistic GST rate that is appropriate and acceptable.

GST Rate Structure

[On 1 July 2017, GST was introduced with an unusually large number of rates. Multiple rates and a very high rate of 28 per cent appeared to have had an adverse announcement effect.] There are separate schedules of rates for goods and services. As is evident from Table 3.1, there are seven schedules of rates for goods, starting from nil to 28 per cent. On the services side, there are six categories of rates, starting from nil to 28 per cent and then a special category where the GST on the supply of services is at the same rate as on the supply of similar goods.

Table 3.1: GST Rate Structure

Rates of Tax on Goods	*Rates of Tax on Services*
Schedule 1: Nil	Services at Nil
Schedule 2: 0.25%	Services at 5%
Schedule 3: 3.0%	Services at 12%
Schedule 4: 5.0%	Services at 18%
Schedule 5: 12%	Services at 28%
Schedule 6: 18%	GST on supply of services at same rate as on supply of similar goods
Schedule 7: 28%	

Source: *GST Booklet*, http://gstcouncil.gov.in/sites/default/files/NOTIFICATION%20PDF/goods-rates-booklet-03July2017.pdf (accessed 4 June 2017).

In Schedule 1, for goods, there are 149 commodities where the GST is nil. GST applied on diamond and precious and semi-precious stones is 0.25 per cent. Goods listed in Schedule 3, with a 3 per cent rate, comprise gold and other precious metals. There are 230 goods that are listed in Schedule 4, with a 5 per cent rate, and 242 in Schedule 5, with a 12 per cent rate. Schedule 6 at 18 per cent has 453 commodities and taxable goods not specified in the other schedules. The 28 per cent rate is applied on 228 items. Similarly, there is a spectrum of services on which different rates have been applied. This rate structure is complex.

In a developing country like India, if tax system reform were to be revenue neutral, if not yield more revenue, and at the same time the decision of economic agents were not to be needlessly interfered with, there is no alternative but to design a system whereby domestic consumption could be taxed comprehensively with a wide base covering goods and services, but without giving rise to the complexities and inefficiencies that mark the existing structure. In this context, the introduction of VAT was historic. However, as the basic objective of the tax system is to make it neutral to trade and business decisions, externally and internally, this could not be done even within the existing VAT design.

GST was introduced to correct such a distortion. In the current regime, GST is characterised by a plethora of exemptions, tax exporting and non-neutrality, with all their ill-effects on economic efficiency and inter-jurisdictional equity. Also, from the consumer's perspective, in the pre-GST regime there were only two VAT rates. Now, with multiple rates, as is evident from Table 3.1, the system has become unduly complex. This may seriously hamper revenue growth and can have adverse growth implications.

Interstate Transactions of Goods and Services

States have accepted the IGST model for taxation of interstate transaction of goods and services as suggested by the Working Group of concerned officials of Central and state governments. In this IGST model,

> Centre would levy IGST which would be CGST plus SGST on all inter-State transactions of taxable goods and services with appropriate provision for consignment or stock transfer of goods and services. The inter-State seller will pay IGST on value addition after adjusting available credit of IGST, CGST, and SGST on his purchases. The Exporting State will transfer to the Centre the credit of SGST used in payment of IGST. The Importing dealer will claim credit of IGST while discharging his output tax liability in his own State. The Centre will transfer to the importing State the credit of IGST used in payment of SGST. The relevant information will also be submitted to the Central Agency which will act as a clearing house mechanism, verify the claims and inform the respective governments to transfer the funds.[2]

Framework for Exemptions, Thresholds and Composition

The turnover thresholds for VAT varied widely across states, from Rs 2 lakh in smaller states to Rs 40 lakh per annum in larger states, along with wide variation in the list of exempted goods across states. Now, in the GST regime, to allow for uniform treatment of interstate transactions nationally, it may be necessary to bridge these variations so that tax cascading is eliminated. However, the concerns of smaller states need to be kept in mind. For this reason, perhaps such convergence could be targeted over a certain period of time rather than immediately.

Under GST, taxpayers with an aggregate turnover of Rs 20 lakh would be exempted from tax. For north-eastern states including Sikkim and other hilly states, the exemption limit is Rs 10 lakh. It is to be noted that aggregate turnover shall include the aggregate value of all taxable and non-taxable/non-GST supplies, exempt/nil-rated supplies and exports of goods and/or services, and exclude taxes under GST. All suppliers are liable to register under GST law in the state from where he/she makes a taxable supply of goods and/or services if his/her aggregate turnover exceeds the aforementioned thresholds. However, certain categories are required to be registered mandatorily, irrespective of the thresholds: persons making any interstate taxable supply (e.g., from Delhi to Maharashtra), casual taxable person (no fixed place where GST is applicable), non-resident taxable person (no fixed place in India), persons who are required to pay tax under reverse charge, persons who are required to deduct tax at source, agents of a supplier, input service distributor, persons who supply goods or services through e-commerce operator, every e-commerce operator (e.g., Flipkart, Amazon), an aggregator who supplies services under his brand name, any specialised agency of the United Nations or any multilateral financial institution.

Any person with an aggregate turnover not exceeding Rs 75 lakh (Rs 50 lakh for north-eastern and hilly states) shall be eligible to pay tax by the composition scheme. The composition scheme is a convenient way for small taxpayers to escape from too many GST formalities and to pay the tax at a fixed rate based on their business turnover. Under this scheme, a taxpayer will pay tax as a percentage of his/her turnover during the financial year without the benefit of input tax credit (ITC). The floor rate of tax for

CGST and SGST shall not be less than 1 per cent. A taxpayer opting for the composition scheme will not collect any tax from his/her customers. When the eligible taxpayer is opting for the composition scheme under GST, he/she has to file summarised returns on a quarterly basis, instead of three monthly returns (as is applicable for normal businesses). The composition scheme will be available only on intra-state supplies.

A Few Operational Issues under GST

Common Approach

The Centre and the states have so far adopted a common framework to implement GST in a similar fashion to make it successful and to achieve its main goal of creating a national common market. This has also been supported by a near common law and a common assessment procedure. As reported in the Central Board of Excise and Customs (CBEC) website:

> The basic features of the returns mechanism in GST include electronic filing of returns, uploading of invoice level information and auto-population of information relating to Input Tax Credit (ITC) from returns of supplier to that of recipient, invoice-level information matching and auto reversal of Input Tax Credit in case of mismatch. The returns mechanism is designed to assist the taxpayer to file returns and avail ITC.[3]

It is further noted that,

> Under GST, a regular taxpayer needs to furnish monthly returns and one annual return. There are separate returns for a taxpayer registered under the composition scheme, nonresident taxpayer, taxpayer registered as an Input Service Distributor, a person liable to deduct or collect the tax (TDS/TCS) and a person granted Unique Identification Number. It is important to note that a taxpayer is not required to file all types of returns. In fact, taxpayers are required to file returns depending on the activities they undertake. All the returns are to be filed online.[4]

As is evident, while there is common return for CGST, SGST and IGST, returns have to be filed on a monthly basis. Monthly returns filing and online matching of ITC remains a major issue. One of the major attractions of the online mechanism as claimed by CBEC was auto-population of information with regard to ITC. This was deferred as the Goods and Services Tax Network (GSTN) was still a work in progress. Many stakeholders raised the serious concern that before shifting to the GST regime, there was a need to develop adequate infrastructure. In the GST model, a system for interstate verification of dealers and transactions is essential to ensure tax compliance and check avoidance. Given the volume of such transactions, this system necessarily had to be based on information technology (IT). For the ease of compliance, there is a need to simplify the process and take corrective steps for speedy redress of grievances like delayed ITC payment and refund to the exporters.

A major challenge to the introduction of GST in the country is building the capacity of the administration to implement the new tax. The tax administration at both the Central and state levels will have to be augmented to deal with the new tax regime. Preparing the administration to implement GST would require considerable effort at building capacity in matters such as the accounting system, forms and procedures, assessment, auditing and computerisation. As per the current status, the GSTN is still a work in progress.

Checkposts

Most states have put in place a system of checkposts on its road borders. Apart from other verifications that may take place, these checkposts verify and document interstate sales of goods carried by the vehicles that cross these borders. These details are then verified with the VAT returns of the importing dealers. The need for such an arrangement to continue in the GST regime has been questioned, especially in view of the abolition of central sales tax (CST). But there are concerns about the possibility of tax arbitrage. The fact remains that such checkposts, by the very nature of operation, generate enormous delays in road traffic, sometimes up to three hours per checkpost. A freight truck travelling by road between Delhi and Chennai will need to cross five state borders and 10 checkposts. Delivery times for goods may be extended significantly because of delays at checkposts. The arrangement also encourages rent-seeking behaviour.

It may be difficult to eliminate checkposts given the various concerns of state governments, which may extend beyond collection of taxes and movement of goods to vehicle fitness examination, prevention of trafficking, collection of local cess, etc. But what appears to be egregious is that the same vehicle has to pass through two checkposts while crossing one border—the exporting state's checkpost and the importing state's checkpost. Both these checkposts are often located within a couple of kilometres of each other, and a vehicle driver has to spend considerable time in both. Perhaps it may be possible for both states to put up a combined checkpost. Officials of both states could sit together and conduct their verifications in one checkpost. Or one state could handle traffic in one direction and the other state in the other direction. But essentially there could be only one check per border for a goods vehicle. Such an arrangement will significantly reduce travel time.

Expanding the Tax Envelope

The construction sector is a significant contributor to the national economy. Housing expenditure dominates personal consumption expenditure. Further, the present piecemeal taxation of this sector encourages perverse incentives. In the pre-GST era, raw material was charged central value-added tax (CENVAT), while the works contract was charged VAT. Stamp duty is still levied on sale even after GST. With no provision of ITC in place, there is little incentive to record such transactions at either the construction stage or the sales stage at their correct value. This leads to substantial loss of tax revenue and fuels the parallel economy. GST also did not consider the inclusion of this sector. However, given the potential long-term benefits to the economy and to a successful

GST, the construction and housing sectors need to be included in the GST tax base during a subsequent phase.

Another possible step to expand the GST tax base will be the inclusion of the rail sector. This will be necessary if a level playing field is to be provided to the road and air transportation sectors, which will be subject to this tax. This inclusion will also ensure that all interstate transportation of goods can be tracked through the proposed IT network. The railways will benefit from this by availing ITC on the significant purchases made by it.

Post-GST Transitional Issues

The government has declared that the remaining part of the financial year 2017–18, i.e., the period post the implementation of GST on 1 July 2017, would be treated as the period of transition, signalling that the government would be prepared to make calibrated changes as the situation unfolds, without a rigid view. But despite the fact that the GST Council has been trying hard to be as clear as possible in drafting rules and conveying them to all stakeholders for the successful implementation of the GST regime, several transition issues need to be addressed for a meaningful transition of this magnitude in our taxation system.

Amongst the several transition issues and implementation challenges being faced by the entire country, the key issue is ensuring the dissemination of symmetric and timely information to all concerned stakeholders. Given the completely new tax regime the country has now adopted, despite several guidelines, circulars and announcements, the lack of clarity on several diverse issues faced by very diverse industries and sectors remains a concern.

Another challenge in the transition phase will be the modification of IT systems to make them GST compliant. The multiplicity of rates, decentralised registration, generation of item-wise invoice with multiple copies, calculation of item-wise GST for multiple slab rates and printing of such invoices containing numerous details have increased the implementation challenge. With no requisite training provided to sellers for undertaking such a mammoth technical upgrade of record-keeping and maintenance before GST implementation, timely and efficient transition from the current to more sophisticated systems of record-keeping, tax charging and tax filing will pose a hindrance for smooth transition.

Yet another concern expressed by the industry immediately after the implementation of GST was the treatment of closing inventory. Although guidelines exist about the treatment of existing input credit and refund claim into the new GST regime, inventory destocking to ensure that they begin on a clean slate with the GST remains challenging. With the raw material, semi-finished goods and finished goods in different stages pre- and post-GST implementation, decisions regarding the pricing pattern of such goods remain an unsolved question. Consumers too are at the receiving end of this transition exercise, with uncertainty regarding pricing affecting buying and spending decisions.

A related transition issue is adherence to the anti-profiteering provisions. The anti-profiteering rules aim to ensure that the benefits of reduction in the rate of taxes on the supply of goods and services or the benefits of ITC by way of reduction in prices is passed on to buyers. However, in the absence of clear guidelines on the manner of computation of profiteering, the industry is finding it difficult to identify the quantum of benefit on the anti-profiteering provisions. This shall definitely lead to some distortionary pricing in the interim period, the consequences of which can be manifold.

Notes

1. For example, earlier, while the Union did not have the right to tax the sale of goods, states could not tax services.
2. https://www.gstindia.com/inter-state-gst-igst-inter-state-transactions/ (accessed 7 June 2018).

3. http://www.cbic.gov.in/resources//htdocs-cbec/gst/Returns.pdf;jsessionid=BCDEC1CBF3DAD3BA60CD02153A921899 (accessed 26 February 2019).
4. http://www.cbic.gov.in/resources//htdocs-cbec/gst/Returns.pdf;jsessionid=BCDEC1CBF3DAD3BA60CD02153A921899 (accessed 26 February 2019).

Four

Making Sense of GST Revenue and Implementation

A Preliminary Assessment

A significant increase in government tax revenue was one of the biggest expectations from the goods and services tax (GST). In other words, GST was expected to be a 'money-spinner'. This is also evident from the GST revenue estimates that the government has made in the budget documents. In the budget of 2018–19, the government expected a revenue from GST—comprising revenue from the central goods and services tax (CGST), integrated goods and services tax (IGST) and GST compensation cess—to the tune of Rs 7,43,900 crore. Despite the fact that in the revised estimate (RE) numbers for the same year, the expected revenue was revised to Rs 6,43,900 crore, the government budgeted Rs 7,61,200 crore in the year 2019–20, on the back of better economic performance and tax compliance. Revenue from GST in this year formed close to 30 per cent of the gross tax revenue of the government. It is, therefore, central to the health of government finances.

We have completed the one-year mark since the successful rollout of GST. As the dust settles on the euphoria around this long-anticipated overhaul of the Indian taxation regime, what is becoming a matter of active academic and public discourse is gauging the performance of GST. On paper and in spirit, with a broader tax base and higher compliance (due to an in-built mechanism for enterprises to register with Goods and Services Tax Network [GSTN]), GST promised higher revenues for the Union and state governments alike. Whether or not GST has boosted revenues remains to be seen. This chapter proposes that while a plethora of revenue figures float around, e.g., the ministry of finance notified that the total revenue collected under GST in the period between August 2017 and March 2018 was Rs 7.19 lakh crore,[1] these are at best indicative of a transitory phase and a process of GST in the making. We suggest that it is too early to evaluate the revenue performance of GST primarily on account of the fact that it is still evolving. We are yet to witness a complete transition from a 'multiple taxes, multiple rate' regime to a 'one nation, one tax' regime. Additionally, the constantly changing compliance structure and the teething problems associated with its implementation make any meaningful assessment of the revenue position post-GST a cumbersome and painstaking exercise.

GST in Making: The Changes in Tax Rates

The GST Council has held 27 meetings till date, with the latest held on 4 May 2018. While 18 of these meetings happened before the rollout of GST, nine meetings have been held since 1 July 2017. It is important to note that discussions and deliberations on the rates for various goods and services to be subsumed under GST were an integral agenda in all the first 18 GST Council meetings. In all meetings, except the 26th GST Council Meet, representations from state governments expressed their dissatisfaction with the extremely high tax rates on certain categories of goods and services. Consequently, rate cuts have been proposed and implemented.[2] Changes in GST rates on goods and services, changes in compensation cess, changes in the IGST rate, addition and deletion of goods and services from the GST exemption list, changes in the input tax credit (ITC) criteria with regard to certain goods, etc., that have found their place in every GST Council meeting reflect that GST has to stand the test of time and accommodate all stakeholders' concerns before it can stabilise and celebrate its coming of age. The finance minister strongly supported the rationalisation process, stating that 'GST broadly has settled down. Almost in every meeting now, we are able to rationalise the tariffs and this process will continue. It will continue with the structure tariffs being rationalised and the structure itself being rationalised as the collections go up' (*The Economic Times* 2018). The constant reshuffling of rates has created a great deal of confusion among businesses, especially smaller businesses, which find it difficult to maintain accounts and remain abreast of the new developments related to such rate changes. Furthermore, complications also arise from the application of differential GST rates on goods and services that are visibly of the same or similar nature. A few such examples are discussed in Box 4.1.

Among the most noteworthy meetings is the 23rd GST Council meeting held on 10 November 2018. The council recommended a reduction in the GST rate from 28 per cent to 18 per cent on goods falling under 178 headings (at the 4-digit level of HSN codes).[3] A pruning of tax rates to this extent and with such wide coverage is expected to impact revenue from GST collections significantly, but to assess whether the adverse effect of shortfall in revenues due to rate cuts would be offset by better compliance and higher demand due to the rate cut is a rather tricky affair. In addition, even though the anti-profiteering clause of GST mandates that any rate cut be passed on to the consumers in the form of lower prices, it is unfair to expect the readiness of businesses to account for this mechanism of anti-profiteering while they are still in a nascent stage in terms of their understanding of the complexities of GST. As a result, making any realistic estimates of GST collections amidst these incessant changes is a challenging task.

GST and Compliance: The Inherent Challenges

It is believed that various built-in mechanisms in the design of GST would make it difficult for businesses to evade taxes. Hence, the improved compliance would boost tax revenue. However, achieving this will likely prove a tough row to hoe, given the many

Box 4.1: One HSN Code, Multiple GST Rates and Different ITC Criteria

While the multiple tax slabs in our present GST are a far cry from an ideal GST, what adds to the complexity of the system are the differential rates of taxes for products under the same broader two-digit Harmonised System Nomenclature (HSN) codes. For instance, footwear having a retail sale price not exceeding Rs 500 a pair, provided the retail price is indelibly marked or embossed on the footwear itself (HSN code 64), is charged at 5 per cent. But products under codes 6401–06 (for instance, 6403, i.e., footwear with outer soles of rubber plastics, leather or composition of leather and uppers of leather) are charged a GST rate of 18 per cent. Similarly, ultra high temperature milk (0401), milk and cream, concentrated or containing added sugar or other sweetening matter, including skimmed milk powder and milk food for babies (0402), are charged at 5 per cent, while condensed milk (0402 91 10, 0402 99 20) is charged at 12 per cent.

Further, there is an additional layer of complexity brought by differential GST rates and ITC criteria on certain services. The decision of the 23rd GST Council Meeting to change the GST rates and ITC eligibility criteria for restaurants circulated vide the press release dated 10 November 2018 could have severe ramifications. The press release stated that:

1. Restaurants in hotel premises having room tariff of less than Rs 7,500 per unit per day will attract GST of 5 per cent without ITC.
2. Restaurants in hotel premises having room tariff of Rs 7,500 and above per unit per day (even for a single room) will attract GST of 18 per cent with full ITC.

When ITC cannot be availed, as in the case of restaurants in hotel premises having room tariff of less than Rs 7,500 per unit per day, the idea of a common market is under threat as the market conditions available to such restaurants are expected to be different from the restaurants in hotel premises having room tariff of Rs 7,500 and above per unit per day (even for a single room), which attract GST of 18 per cent and can avail full ITC.

Such differential ITC eligibility criteria and GST rates for a broad class of goods and services are conceptually in contradiction with the envisaged GST structure.

Source: http://www.cbic.gov.in/resources//htdocs-cbec/gst/gst-services-23rd%20GST-Council.pdf (accessed 19 July 2018).

challenges that the system faces. While some of these compliance-related challenges are part of the teething process and will cease to exist with time, a few challenges that plague the system are a result of problems in the very design of the compliance structure of GST.

As on 1 May 2018, the total number of registered taxpayers stood at 10.85 million, of which 6.4 million (out of 6.6 million total migrated businesses) are the ones that have had a complete migration from the previous tax regime and 4.4 million (out of 5.1 million) are the ones that applied for new registration and are approved.[4] Of these 10.85 million taxpayers registered with GST, 2.01 million have opted for the composition scheme. There has been a significant rise in the total registered taxpayers under GST from July 2017 to May 2018, and the rising share of new registrants (the figures have more than doubled in this period, from 19.4 per cent to 40.7 per cent) suggests that GST is aiding formalisation (Figure 4.1). There has also been a doubling of the proportion of registered taxpayers who are opting for the composition scheme.

Figure 4.1: Registered Taxpayers under GST

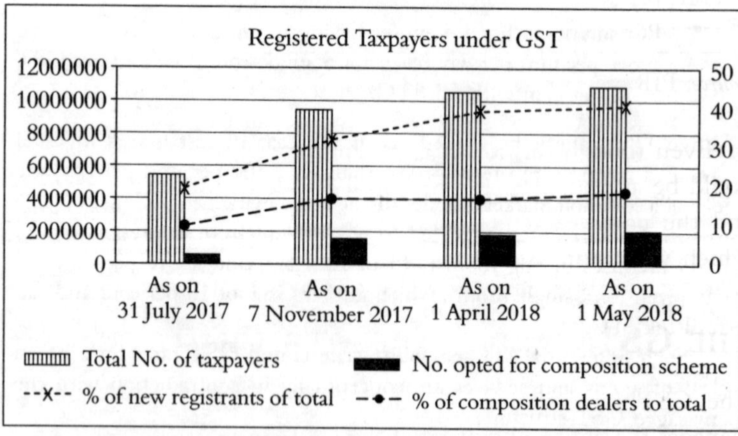

Source: 'GST—Concept and Status' (2018), https://cbec-gst.gov.in/pdf/01052018-GST-Concept-Status.pdf (accessed 11 June 2018).

It is of paramount importance that the IT infrastructure be efficient enough to accommodate these millions of businesses and the manifold returns that they shall file. The monthly figures of eligible taxpayers and taxpayers who filed returns show that while the proportion of taxpayers who filed returns has increased by 8.57 per cent from July 2017 to March 2018, post-December 2018, when the figures reached a high of 66 per cent, there has been a gradual decline (Figure 4.2).

Figure 4.2: Monthly Returns Filing Figures

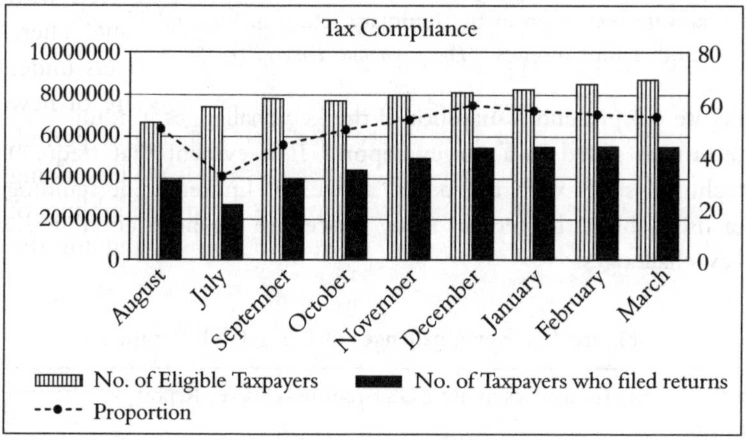

Source: PIB press release, dated 27 April 2018.

Even though this needs to be monitored, part of the decline could be attributed to the technical problems in the IT interface and the complex (and changing) returns filing system, both of which would impede the returns filing process.

THE GSTN AND ASSOCIATED CHALLENGES

The GSTN is a non-profit, non-government organisation that manages the entire IT system of the GST portal. With the rollout of GST on 1 July 2017, the major cause for concern shared by most stakeholders was the IT preparedness of the system as well as the IT literacy level of the users. The apprehensions indeed turned out to be true, as is evident from the shared experiences of users with the GSTN that continue to find prominent space in leading dailies, newsrooms and other social media platforms.

> The industry experienced significant issues with the GSTN system, such as inability of taxpayers to access the GSTN system, extremely slow response rate of the system and slow response time for resolving various errors faced by the taxpayers for their respective returns, no facility to rectify the inadvertent errors in the returns etc. This led to repeated extensions of the due dates for compliances and also the extension of the summary return in form GSTR 3B for another four months. (*The Economic Times* 2017a)

Figure 4.3 presents a snapshot of the key challenges in filing GST returns as stated in a survey report.[5] It is evident that frequent technical snags with the portal as well as limited understanding of users about the returns filing procedure are both cited as the key challenges.

Figure 4.3: Key Challenges in Filing GST Returns

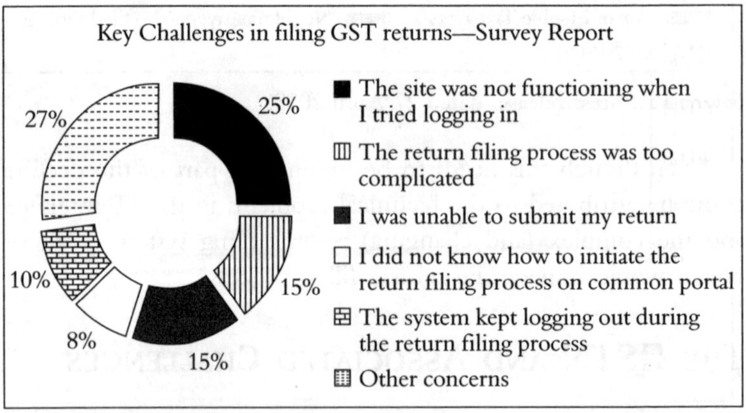

Source: Minutes of the 23rd GST Council Meeting, http://www.gstcouncil.gov.in/sites/default/files/Minutes/Signed%20Minutes%20-%2023rd%20GST%20Council%20Meeting.pdf (accessed 12 June 2018).

It is also important to examine the mode chosen by businesses to upload invoices (outward supplies with regard to filing GSTR-1). Figure 4.4 suggests that roughly three-fourths of businesses prefer to use the offline portal to prepare the returns and then upload them. Only 17 per cent users avail the services of the GST Suvidha Provider (GSP), while a miniscule 8 per cent of users use a web-based mode to directly file their returns on the GST common portal. It is also important to note that the rate of rejection is the highest for users using the services of GSP to upload invoices. While 29 per cent of the total invoices uploaded using GSP are rejected, the rate of rejection is 22 per cent for users using the offline mode and a paltry 0.03 per cent for users using the web-based mode.

Additionally, in the 24th GST Council Meeting, while discussing issues related to the introduction of a nationwide e-way bill system, it was pointed out that one of the reasons for the delay was the inability to procure a software licence despite the timely

Figure 4.4: Choice of Mode for Uploading Invoices to File GSTR-1

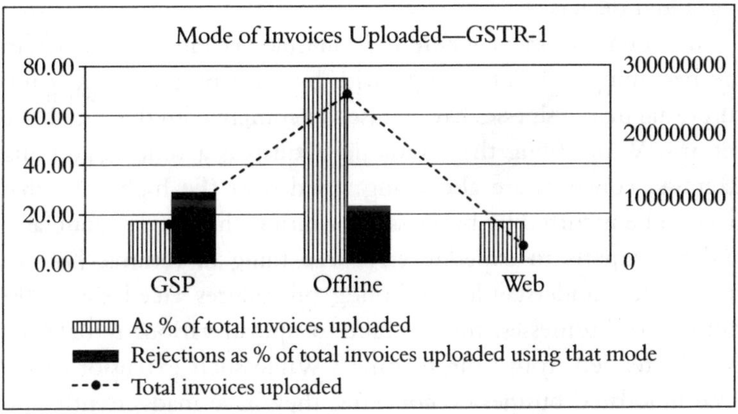

Source: Minutes of the 22nd GST Council Meeting, http://gstcouncil.gov.in/sites/default/files/Minutes/Signed%20Minutes%20-%20 22nd%20GST%20Council%20Meeting.pdf (accessed 12 June 2018).

installation of the requisite hardware. All these issues point out the loopholes in the technical infrastructure that forms the backbone of GST. With such compliance-related issues plaguing the GST system at present, it is difficult to get any realistic estimate of the economic activity and the GST revenue thereof.

Multiple Returns and Multiple Delays in Deadlines for Filing Returns

The initial compliance structure proposed that a normal business file 37 returns annually—monthly GSTR-1 with regard to outward supplies, monthly GSTR-2 with regard to inward supplies, monthly GSTR-3 with regard to finalisation of tax returns and actual tax amount, and an annual return via GSTR-9. For the interim period, a provisional return—GSTR-3B—has to be filed by these businesses. For businesses opting for the composition scheme (more on it later in this section), five returns have to be filed in a year—quarterly GSTR-4 and an annual GSTR-9A. There are other GST returns as well—GSTR-5, GSTR-6, GSTR-7, GSTR-8, GSTR-10 and GSTR-11—with respect to specific registered dealers.

In an environment where the multiple tax rates in the system are becoming difficult to cope with by most businesses, it is not surprising that businesses have refused to comply with these multiple returns. While filing these multiple returns is a time-consuming exercise, concerns are also being raised over the high costs that have to be incurred by businesses for hiring chartered accountants and tax experts to expedite error-free filing of returns. Due to the limited understanding of filing procedures faced by a vast number of businesses, the deadline to upload various returns has been extended from time to time.[6] While such extensions have accommodated businesses' concerns, they have inadvertently also created confusion among businesses about the revised deadlines, despite the various press releases issued by the Central Board of Excise and Customs (CBEC) and efforts of other outreach media. A simple user-friendly returns filing process that does not entail high time and financial cost to registered businesses would ensure better compliance, and hence higher revenues.

Taking cognisance of the persisting problems related to the GSTN and the concerns raised by businesses about filing returns, corrective steps have been taken by the government. In the 26th Meeting of the GST Council, the members discussed the possible simplification in the GST returns filing procedure. As a result, in the recently concluded 27th GST Council Meeting, many measures were taken towards simplification of GSTR filing and an easy IT interface, the most noteworthy being the decision to allow all taxpayers (excluding a few exceptions, like composition dealers) to file only one monthly return.[7] It is expected that the remaining challenges will be promptly addressed to facilitate user-friendly and timely compliance that shall, in turn, provide a boost to revenue collections.

GST and the Turnover Limit

Businesses with a turnover of below Rs 20 lakh have been kept outside the GST net (for special category states, except Jammu and Kashmir, enumerated in Article 279A of the Constitution, the threshold exemption limit is fixed at Rs 10 lakh). The GST Council also recommended a composition scheme for small taxpayers—registered businesses with a turnover limit of Rs 75 lakh and Rs 50 lakh for special category states enumerated in Article 279A of the Constitution, except Jammu and Kashmir and Uttarakhand—who can get rid of tedious GST formalities and pay GST at a fixed rate of turnover. This turnover limit for the composition scheme was further raised to Rs 1 crore (Rs 75 lakh for special category states, except Jammu and Kashmir and Uttarakhand). The *Economic Survey 2017–18* (Ministry of Finance 2018) noted that the distribution of turnover is highly skewed—below threshold firms filed 32 per cent of total returns but their share of tax liability was less than 1 per cent, while large firms (with an annual turnover of more than Rs 100 crore) filed only 0.6 per cent of the total returns, but their share in tax liability stood at 54 per cent. These figures suggest two things: (a) while GST could bring informal firms under the tax net, their share in the total tax liability would be miniscule given their relatively small annual turnover; (b) the real challenge is to correct the regressive and skewed tax structure whereby larger firms that have a disproportionately higher share in the total tax liability constitute only a small percentage of the total taxpayers. Concerted efforts on the latter will play a crucial role in mobilising tax revenues under the present GST framework.

In light of these findings, we examine data from the returns filed under GSTR-1, GSTR-2 and GSTR-3B. Data collated from GSTR-1 and GSTR-3B paint a picture similar to the one reported in the *Economic Survey 2017–18* (Figure 4.5). The data suggests that registered businesses with an annual turnover of less than Rs 1.5 crore (suggested revised threshold for the composition scheme) filed 80.12 per cent of total returns, while their share

Figure 4.5: Compliance in GST: Data from GSTR-1 and GSTR-3B

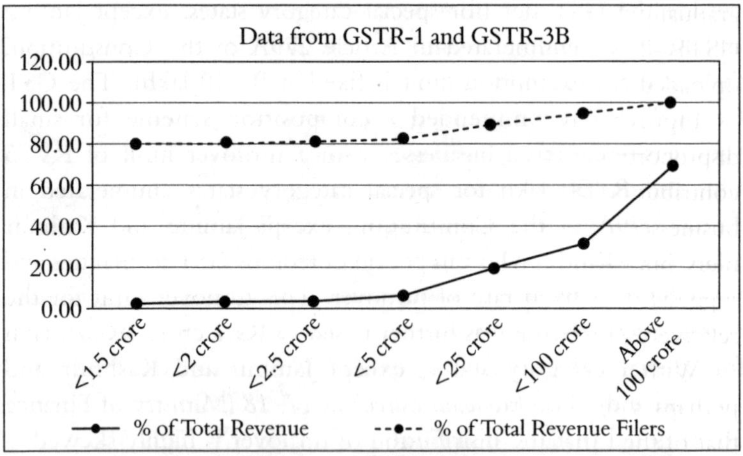

Source: Minutes of the 23rd GST Council Meeting, http://www.gstcouncil.gov.in/sites/default/files/Minutes/Signed%20Minutes%20-%2023rd%20GST%20Council%20Meeting.pdf (accessed 12 June 2018).

in the total revenue was only 5.58 per cent. On the other side of the spectrum, larger firms with an annual turnover of more than Rs 100 crore had roughly 70 per cent share in total revenues, but constituted only 5.69 per cent of total GST return filers. Registered businesses with an annual turnover of up to Rs 5 crore constitute 85 per cent of total return filers, with their share in total revenue being just a little over 10 per cent.

Given this skewed structure, an upward revision of the turnover limit for the composition scheme may ensure further simplification of GST compliance. This revision, at the same time, would help smaller businesses to avoid the complexities of GST compliance. This would also reduce the traffic on the GSTN, which may go a long way in improving the technical efficiency of the IT interface and GST compliance.

Matching the number of taxpayers auto-drafted from GSTR-1 to those who actually submit GSTR-2 reveals two interesting findings: (a) a large proportion of total taxpayers upload up to 50 invoices, and as the number of invoices being uploaded increase (a proxy of firm size), the proportion of taxpayers who file GSTR-2 gradually decreases; (b) the share of taxpayers who actually submit GSTR-2 is inversely related to the number of invoices being uploaded (Figure 4.6).

Figures 4.5 and 4.6 suggest that larger businesses are disproportionately smaller in the number of returns filed, while their contribution to taxes is more than 70 per cent. The small registered businesses make up for more than 80 per cent of total GST return filers, but contribute less than 10 per cent to the total revenue. This suggests that while tax contribution is low, compliance pressure relative to turnover is greater for small business.

With such a skewed structure of revenue source in place, perhaps a revision of the GST exemption threshold along with that of the turnover limit for the composition scheme may ensure further simplification of GSTN compliance. This would also reduce the traffic on the GSTN, which may go a long way in improving the technical efficiency of the IT interface and GST compliance. In the 23rd GST Council meeting, a recommendation was made to

Figure 4.6: Compliance in GST: Data from GSTR-1 and GSTR-2

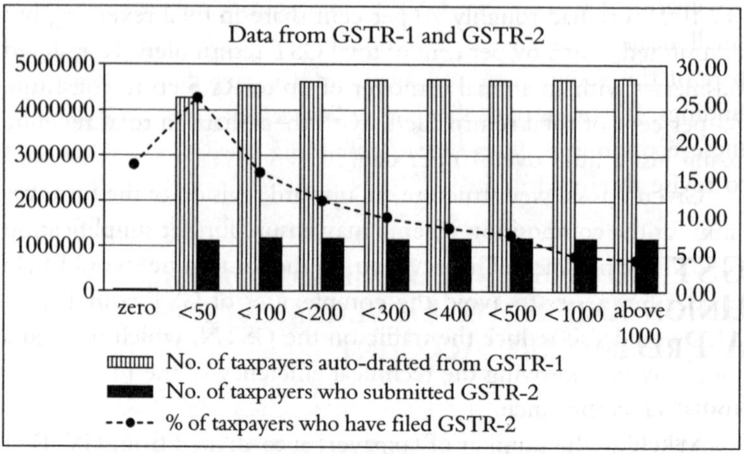

Source: Minutes of the 23rd GST Council Meeting, http://www.gstcouncil.gov.in/sites/default/files/Minutes/Signed%20Minutes%20-%2023rd%20GST%20Council%20Meeting.pdf (accessed 12 June 2018).

increase the annual turnover eligibility for the composition scheme under the CGST/SGST law to Rs 2 crore from the present limit of Rs 1 crore by amending Section 10(1) of the CGST and SGST Acts, and to increase the annual turnover threshold for composition to Rs 1.5 crore after the amendment in law.

However, one needs to weigh the possible benefits against the likely costs before making any such amendments to the CGST/SGST Acts. The *Economic Survey 2017–18* (Ministry of Finance 2018) pointed out that more than 54.3 per cent of those eligible to register under the composition scheme chose instead to be regular filers. One of the main reasons for this is that businesses registered under the composition scheme cannot avail ITC on their business transactions with large businesses.[8] While the rationale before the introduction of GST was that small dealers who sell directly to consumers (B2C) would opt for the composition scheme, the *Economic Survey* data shows that businesses with an annual turnover of under Rs 1 crore (those eligible to opt for the composition scheme) have almost equal B2B and B2C transactions. In such a scenario, it is clear that GST provides an opportunity to these small dealers, who tend to transact with large traders to be a part of the value chain and avail input tax credits. Given these findings, it is important that the policymakers take cognisance of these economic realities before amending the CGST/SGST Act to revise threshold limits.

GST and Revenue Position of the Union and State Governments: A Preliminary Account

Insofar as the revenues from SGST and CGST are concerned, at best a sketchy account is available that can help us understand where state and Union governments stand after nine-and-a-half months of implementation of GST. We have used the Union budget papers and the Controller General of Accounts (CGA) monthly reports to study the revenue performance of the Centre, and state budget papers along with Comptroller and Auditor General of India (CAG) state accounts (monthly key indicators) to assess states' revenue position after the implementation of GST.

GST and the Union Government

With respect to the Union government, the Union budget 2018–19 estimated the total GST revenue for 2017–18 to be around Rs 4,44,631 crore—Rs 2,21,400 crore from CGST collection, Rs 1,61,900 from IGST collection[9] and Rs 61,331 crore from compensation cess. By 2018–19, the total GST collections are budgeted to rise to Rs 7,43,900 crore, an increase of 67 per cent from the previous year, mostly on account of higher CGST collections that are expected to gallop to Rs 6,03,900 crore (Figure 4.7). It is to be noted that such a significant increase is expected due to the recent changes in GST. Also, the estimates of 2017–18 pertain to GST collection of only 11 months.

Figure 4.7: Total GST Revenue of the Union Government (in Rs crore)

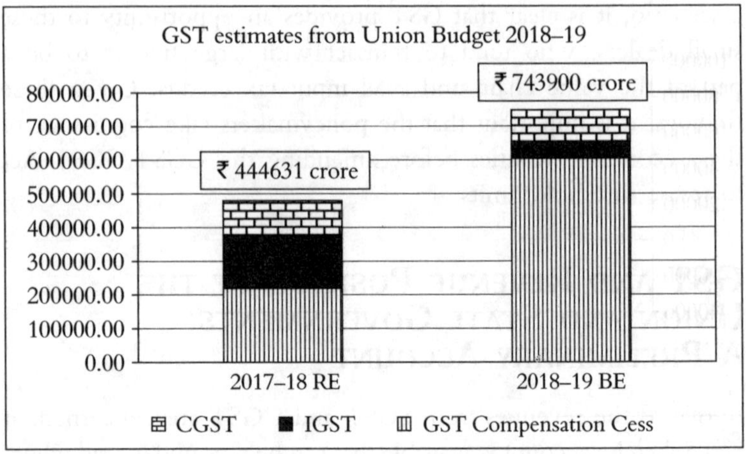

Source: Union government budget, 2018–19.

Given these estimates, we analysed the monthly GST collections of the Union government for the past year, i.e., 2017–18, from the monthly CAG reports. It is noted that till March 2018, CGST collections stood at Rs 4,34,672 crore, of which CGST collections stood at Rs 2,03,262 crore, IGST Rs 1,68,814 crore and compensation cess Rs 62,596 crore (Figure 4.8). The collections of the fiscal year 2017–18 also suggest that there has been a shortfall of Rs 9,959 crore in the Union government's GST collections from the estimated amount. While the revenue from IGST and compensation cess exceeded the revised estimated figures, the shortfall has been due to inadequate CGST collections.

Examining the monthly CGST collections (Figure 4.9) reveals that the CGST collections do not display a particular trend that could be utilised for making any projections for the next fiscal year. Given that the introduction of GST completely revamped the Indian taxation system and ever since its rollout it has been subject to constant tweaking, it would be erroneous to draw any meaningful conclusions till the time it stabilises.

Figure 4.8: Union Government Monthly GST Revenue Collection (in Rs crore)

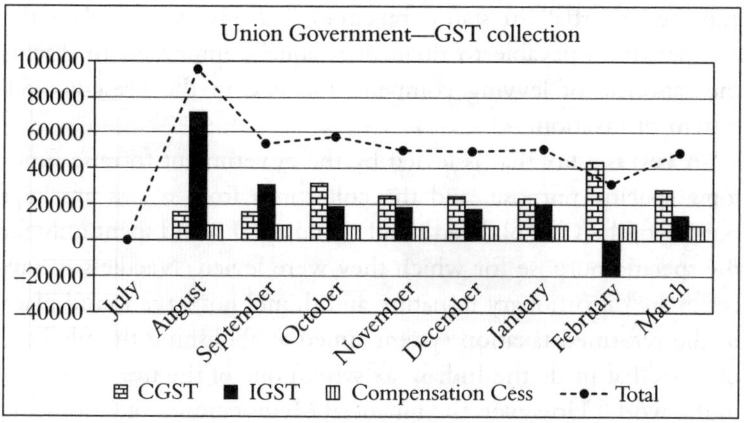

Source: CAG monthly reports, 2017–18.

Figure 4.9: Union Government Monthly CGST Revenue Collection (in Rs crore)

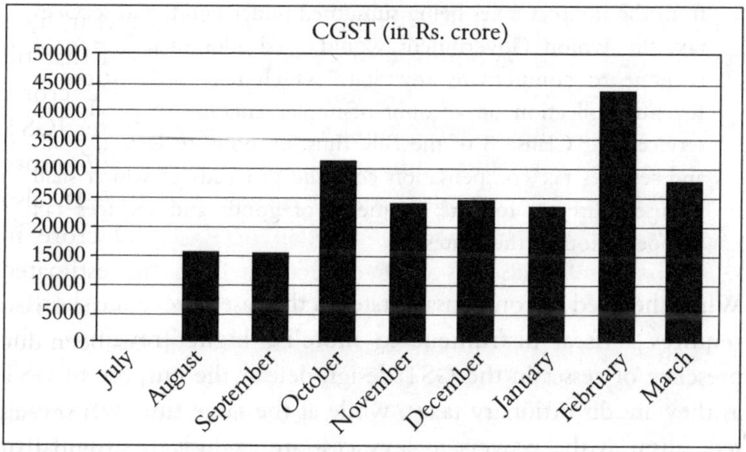

Source: CAG monthly reports, 2017–18.

GST and Compensation Cess

With respect to the compensation cess, it is to be observed that the budgeted amount for 2018–19 is Rs 90,000 crore, an increase of 47 per cent from the 2017–18 estimated amount of Rs 61,331 crore. In this context, while it is pertinent to first estimate the expected shortfall in states' revenues,[10] if any, to calculate the compensation payable to them, it is equally important to discuss the rationale of levying compensation cess in the present GST system of taxation.

A cess is a tax that is levied by the government to raise funds for a specific purpose, and the collections from a cess are kept outside of the Consolidated Fund of India (CFI) and spent only for the specific purpose for which they were levied. Needless to say, cesses are distortionary in nature and should not have found place in the reformed taxation system aimed at abolishing the plethora of taxes that made the Indian tax system one of the most complex in the world. However, the Financial Memorandum of Goods and Services Tax (Compensation to States) Bill, 2017, states that

> since the central goods and services tax rate shall be arrived at so as to protect the present revenues of the Union Government from the indirect taxes being subsumed under goods and services tax, the Union Government would need additional source of revenue to compensate any State which may suffer drop in revenue collection on account of implementation of goods and services tax. Clause 8 of the Bill, thus, proposes to levy a goods and services tax compensation cess, the proceeds of which shall be used directly for the payments of goods and services tax compensation to the States.

While the need to compensate states in the case of revenue shortfall requires a fiscal instrument to mobilise higher revenues, the presence of cesses in the GST design defeats the purpose of GST as they are distortionary taxes, while at the same time weakening federalism as the powers to levy cess are exclusively assigned to the Union government.[11]

Before coming to the provision of cesses in GST design, we first examine how the Union government has been using this fiscal instrument to finance its budgetary requirements. Data from 2010–11 to 2018–19 (BE) reveals that cesses and surcharges have become an important revenue mobilisation instrument (Table 4.1). In absolute terms, cesses and surcharges have more than doubled during 2010–11 to 2016–17, and their rate of growth has outpaced that of the total tax revenue. The share of cesses and surcharges combined in the Union government's total revenue is budgeted at an all-time high of 12.24 per cent in 2018–19, almost double of the share in 2010–11.

Out of the total cess collected by the government, cess collected for financing primary, secondary and higher education expenditure in particular forms a significant share of the total pool. The combined education cess is budgeted at Rs 49,462 crore, almost double of the amount collected by the Centre in 2010–11 (Table 4.1). This share is, however, budgeted to decline to 27.88 per cent (from 62.96 per cent in 2010–11) primarily because service tax and Union excise duties (on which cess was levied) have been subsumed under GST, while the government has announced its intention to abolish the education cess and the secondary and higher education cess on imports in the 2018–19 budget.

While revenues being mobilised by the government by levying cess on goods and services have undoubtedly risen over the years, their utilisation to finance specific expenditure has remained a cause for concern. In the report of the Comptroller and Auditor General of India (CAG 2017) for the year 2016–17, gross irregularities and opaqueness in utilisation of cesses (including research and development cess, education cess and clean energy cess) were flagged by the CAG.

> Against the total collection of Rs 83,497 crore as Secondary and Higher Education Cess (SHEC) in the Consolidated Fund of India during 2006-07 to 2016-17, no amount could be transferred to the earmarked fund in Public Account as neither the schemes were identified on which the cess proceeds were to be spent nor the designated fund was opened in the Public Account to deposit the proceeds of SHEC.

Given the irregularities reported in the utilisation of cess, the proposal to abolish the education cess and the secondary and

Table 4.1: Cess and Surcharge Levied by the Union Government
(in Rs crore)

Year	*Total Cess and Surcharge* (1)	*Total Tax Revenue* (2)	*As % of Total Tax Revenue* (1)/(2)	*Total Education Cess* (3)	*Total Cess* (4)	*As % of Total Cess* (3)/(4)
2010–11	49,628	7,93,072	6.26	25,166	39,971	62.96
2011–12	58,630	8,89,176	6.59	27,194	42,825	63.50
2012–13	60,632	10,36,234	5.85	30,572	52,756	57.95
2013–14	71,714	11,38,734	6.30	33,280	56,989	58.40
2014–15	75,533	12,44,885	6.07	35,977	58,797	61.19
2015–16	83,998	14,55,648	5.77	28,022	63,116	44.40
2016–17	1,26,664	17,15,822	7.38	30,248	1,00,908	29.98
2017–18 BE	1,69,662	19,11,579	8.88	31,654	1,09,364	28.94
2017–18 RE	1,37,063	19,46,119	7.04	29,138	71,315	40.86
2018–19 BE	2,78,029	2,27,1242	12.24	49,462	1,77,424	27.88

Source: Author's calculation using data from Union government budget papers.

higher education cess on imported goods and replace it with a social welfare surcharge (at the rate of 10 per cent of the aggregate duties of customs on imported goods) to provide for the social welfare schemes of the government (finance education, housing and social security) rings a bell of caution. Seen in this light, the presence of distortionary taxes like cesses and surcharges in the GST design needs to be further scrutinised.

The Goods and Services Tax (Compensation to States) Act, 2017 provides for payment of compensation to the states for loss of revenue arising on account of implementation of GST.[12] Thus, the second concern is about estimating states' expected revenue shortfall. But before undertaking this exercise, we present a brief overview of states' revenue position after implementation of GST.

GST and State Governments

The revenue position of states is a bit unclear mostly due to non-availability of data for most states. It is to be noted that only 10 out of a total 29 states, namely Andhra Pradesh, Assam, Bihar, Haryana, Karnataka, Mizoram, Sikkim, Tamil Nadu, Uttar Pradesh and West Bengal, have published their monthly SGST revenue collections in the public domain.[13] Even among these 10 states, only four—Andhra Pradesh, Haryana, Tamil Nadu and Uttar Pradesh—have data for GST from July 2017 onwards. It is important to take cognisance of the fact that irregular and incomplete reporting of SGST revenues by most states impedes efforts to undertake a comprehensive study of states' finances, especially their revenue position. Nonetheless, it is important to take stock of these monthly collections. Figure 4.10 presents the actual SGST collections up to March 2018.[14] As is evident, the states' SGST collections do not point towards any discernible trend that can help us project revenue figures for the coming months.

If we examine month-wise SGST revenues, we find that the SGST revenue collections are sporadic (Figure 4.11) and actually

Figure 4.10: State-wise SGST Revenue Collection (in Rs crore)

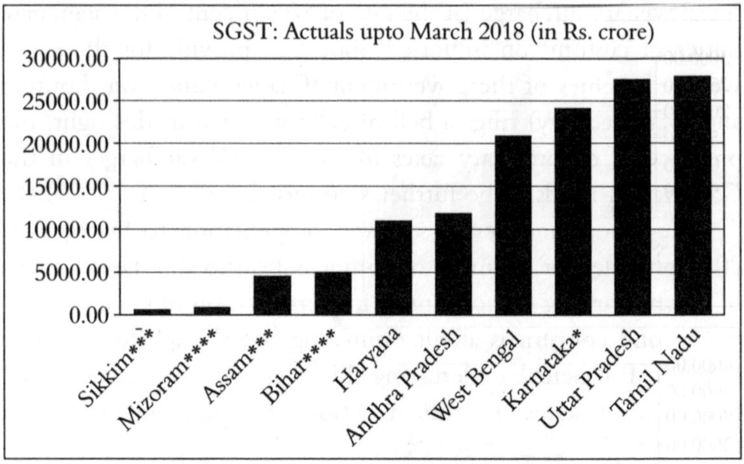

Note: *, **, *** and **** represent revenue figures from August 2017, September 2017, October 2017 and November 2017, respectively.
Source: CAG monthly state accounts.

reflect the changing GST structure that renders instability to revenue collection. It is also to be noted that unlike the reporting of Union government revenues that bifurcates total GST revenues into CGST, IGST and Compensation Cess, none of these states (except Sikkim) have provided such a bifurcation. This makes a true assessment of GST revenue collection by states an incomplete exercise.

Coming back to estimating states' revenue for estimating the revenue shortfall post-GST, if any, we have taken states' sales tax revenue collections as a proxy for the taxes that have been subsumed under GST.[15] Our calculations suggest that historically, states' sales taxes, at an average, have grown at less than 14 per cent per annum (Table 4.2). However, the average rate of growth of states' revenues from SGST and sales tax (that has been subsumed under GST) collections estimated at 14.95 per cent for 2017–18 and 15.61 per cent for 2018–19 suggests that states expect a buoyant economic environment that shall provide a fillip to their SGST

Figure 4.11: Month-wise SGST Revenues for Four States
(in Rs crore)

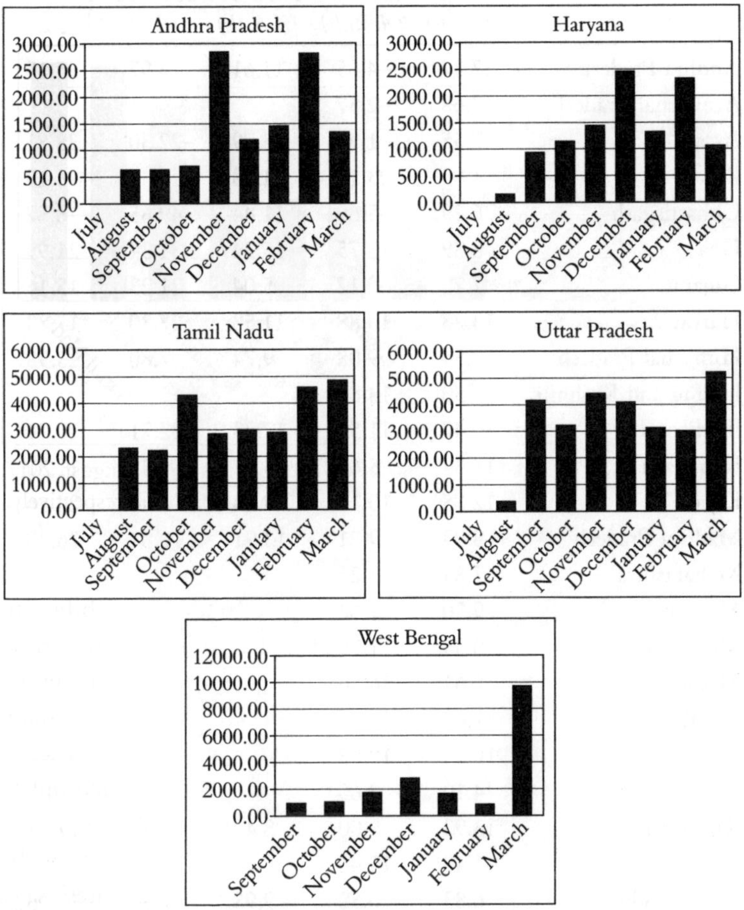

Source: CAG monthly state accounts.

collections, which in turn may not necessitate the payment of compensation cess from the Union government.

While it is too early to make any accurate assessment of states' revenue position, the provisional revenue figures on GST released by a few states reveal that while a few states have collected more

Table 4.2: Sales Tax and GST Growth Rate (in %)

	2014–15 (Actuals)	*2015–16 (Actuals)*	*2016–17 (Actuals)*	*2017–18 (RE)*	*2018–19 (BE)*
Andhra Pradesh	–37.37	–4.65	11.61	17.97	25.10
Arunachal Pradesh	–12.68	–2.57			
Assam	7.35	1.94	16.79	–22.30	28.81
Bihar	1.82	23.19	11.98		–6.19
Chhattisgarh	6.29	5.69	11.44	49.65	6.82
Goa	8.89	13.75	15.24	31.34	21.99
Gujarat	7.73	–0.12	5.04	21.23	13.16
Haryana	13.23	10.88	11.53	27.30	17.73
Himachal Pradesh	16.54	9.08	9.74	7.80	13.98
Jammu and Kashmir	0.50	14.67			
Jharkhand	10.47	11.52	17.23	32.71	10.71
Karnataka	13.54	5.65	13.98	5.35	11.30
Kerala	12.15	10.13	8.84	16.40	20.16
Madhya Pradesh	8.93	9.21	13.91	10.84	26.40
Maharashtra	7.89	3.25			
Manipur	9.50	7.66			
Meghalaya	0.35	11.79			
Mizoram	15.61	16.56			
Nagaland	17.62	11.65			
Odisha	10.14	10.83			
Punjab	4.10	2.60			
Rajasthan	13.93	9.00	8.40	9.25	17.31
Sikkim	–1.48	15.46			
Tamil Nadu	6.83	0.58	9.93	17.34	17.06
Telangana		34.93	14.70	26.33	23.66
Tripura	8.69	16.34			
Uttar Pradesh	11.46	11.72	8.79	10.26	24.99
Uttarakhand	8.30	11.08			
West Bengal	9.53	8.44	7.42	–22.24	–7.58
Average	6.42	9.66	11.56	14.95	15.61

Source: Author's calculation using data from states' finance accounts and states' budget papers.

Figure 4.12: Sales Tax and GST Revenue Collection of a Few States

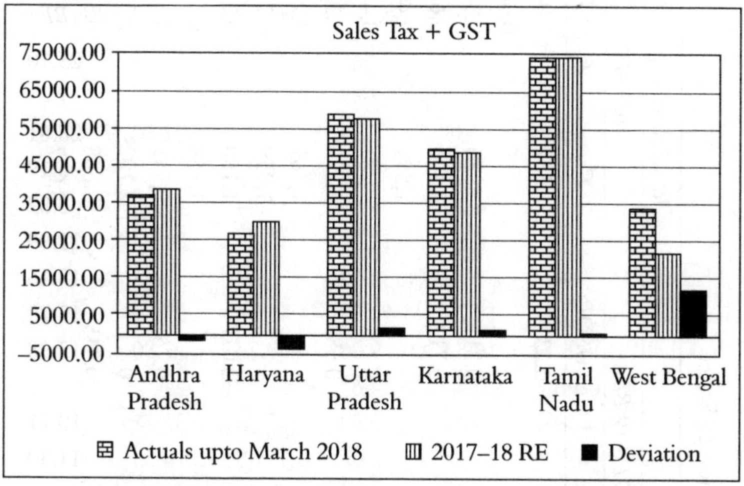

Source: Author's calculations using data from states' budget papers and CAG monthly state accounts.

revenue from GST and sales tax in 2017–18 than the estimated figures, a few have missed the mark (Figure 4.12). For instance, West Bengal has reported GST collections to the tune of Rs 20,645 crore till March 2018, Rs 12,375 crore higher than the estimated amount.

The Union government collected compensation cess worth Rs 62,596 crore in the last fiscal year, out of which it transferred Rs 47,843 crore (roughly three-fourths of the amount) to the states till March 2018.[16] From Table 4.3, it is evident that some states have performed well in their GST collections, and as such, the compensation received by them from the Union is low. Such states include Arunachal Pradesh, Manipur and Sikkim. However, there are significant laggards in Karnataka, Gujarat, Maharashtra and Bihar, which have received almost 41 per cent of the total GST compensation. Still, almost Rs 14,753 crore collected in the name of GST compensation cess remains with the Union. While some have cautioned that the accumulation of the undisbursed

Table 4.3: GST Compensation to States

States	*State Budgets*				*Actual Receipts from GoI*	
	2017–18 RE		*2018–19 BE*		*2017–18*	
	Rs Crore	*% of GSDP*	*Rs Crore*	*% of GSDP*	*Rs Crore*	*% of GSDP*
Andhra Pradesh	1,000	0.126	2,000	0.23	382	0.048
Arunachal Pradesh					15	0.062
Assam	1,000	0.35	1,000	0.311	980	0.345
Bihar	0	0	3,698	0.717	3,140	0.673
Chhattisgarh					1,589	0.484
Goa					281	0.4
Gujarat	4,984.29	0.378	1,0295.7	0.688	4,277	0.324
Haryana					1,461	0.24
Himachal Pradesh					1,059	0.76
Jammu & Kashmir	1,616.13	1.147	3,174.89	2.017	1,160	0.823
Jharkhand					1,368	0.49
Karnataka	6,130	0.483	10,800	0.767	7,535	0.594
Kerala	0	0	0	0	2,102	0.306
Madhya Pradesh	2,200	0.319	2600	0.315	2,668	0.377
Maharashtra					3,077	0.121

(Contd)

(*Table 4.3 contd*)

States	*State Budgets*				*Actual Receipts from GoI*	
	2017–18 RE		*2018–19 BE*		*2017–18*	
	Rs Crore	*% of GSDP*	*Rs Crore*	*% of GSDP*	*Rs Crore*	*% of GSDP*
Manipur					24	0.101
Meghalaya					140	0.447
Mizoram						0
Nagaland						0
Odisha	0.01	0	0.01	0	2,264	0.544
Punjab					4,618	0.967
Rajasthan	3,500	0.417	4,500	0.479	2,899	0.345
Sikkim	0	0	110.58	0.478	6	0.029
Tamil Nadu	970	0.068	1,698.28	0.085	632	0.038
Telangana	1,200	0.16	1500	0.178	169	0.023
Tripura					149	0.328
Uttar Pradesh	1,955	0.142	5,941.51	0.389	2,432	0.182
Uttarakhand					1,432	0.658
West Bengal	4,744.5	0.465	9,876	0.942	1,608	0.152
All States	29,299.93	0.18	57,194.97	0.31	47,467	0.286

Source: State budget documents (2018–19); primary data collected from the Ministry of Finance, Government of India.

compensation cess by the Union government to the states would have adverse macroeconomic consequences and have suggested a reduction of rates (both compensation cess rates and GST 28 per cent slab rates), our analysis suggests that GST is still evolving, and it is too premature to demand any such prompt revisions in rates without giving GST adequate time to stabilise, as this might not yield expected outcomes.

Thus, it is evident that the budgeted revenue estimates are at best indicative of governments' perception of GST and what revenue it shall generate for the states. One therefore needs to study the revenue figures from GST collections with caution, as the new taxation system is still evolving, when addressing the complex ground realities of the Indian economy.

The other complex issue is the apportionment and treatment of IGST. IGST, as per the GST Act, is to be applied on the supply of any good and/or service in the course of interstate supply. The Centre is levying and collecting IGST on all interstate supply of goods and services. The proceeds of IGST are then apportioned between the states and the Centre, under the proposed Article 269A, as provided by the Parliament by law on the recommendations of the GST Council. Further, the CGST collected by the Central government as well as the Union's share of IGST collected is devolved to the states as per the provisions of Article 270.

It is evident from Table 4.4 that a large part of the IGST revenue is shared with the states based on the devolution principle recommended by the Fourteenth Finance Commission. It was supposed to be apportioned on the place of supply. This is indicative of the fact that the IT system in operation to track transactions needs to be strengthened further to resolve this issue of allocation based on the devolution formula instead of place of supply.

Table 4.4: Making Sense of IGST Data from State Budgets

IGST	*2017–18 RE*			*2018–19 BE*		
States	*OTR*	*Devolution*	*Total*	*OTR*	*Devolution*	*Total*
Andhra Pradesh	2,92,731.00		2,92,731.00	90,405.00		90,405.00
Arunachal Pradesh		1,08,495.00	1,08,495.00		45,642.00	45,642.00
Assam		2,25,141.00	2,25,141.00	5,81,147.00	69,531.00	65,0678.00
Bihar		6,57,201.00	6,57,201.00		2,02,965.00	2,02,965.00
Chhattisgarh	4,24,092.00		4,24,092.00	7,14,431.20		7,14,431.20
Goa		25,703.00	25,703.00		7,938.00	7,938.00
Gujarat		2,09,706.00	2,09,706.00		64,764.00	64,764.00
Haryana			0.00			0.00
Himachal Pradesh		48,483.00	48,483.00		17,018.31	17,018.31
Jammu & Kashmir			0.00			0.00
Jharkhand			0.00			0.00
Karnataka		3,20,474.00	3,20,474.00		98,973.00	98,973.00
Kerala			0.00			0.00
Madhya Pradesh		5,13,249.00	5,13,249.00		1,58,508.00	1,58,508.00
Maharashtra	8,88,804.00		8,88,804.00	15,16,276.00		15,16,276.00

(*Contd*)

(*Table 4.4 contd*)

IGST	*2017–18 RE*			*2018–19 BE*		
States	*OTR*	*Devolution*	*Total*	*OTR*	*Devolution*	*Total*
Manipur			24,301.01			29,161.21
Meghalaya		43,655.00	43,655.00		26,138.00	26,138.00
Mizoram		31,279.00	31,279.00		18,723.00	18,723.00
Nagaland			33,863.00			13,062.00
Odisha		3,15,647.00	3,15,647.00		97,482.00	97,482.00
Punjab		1,07,233.00	1,07,233.00		33,117.00	33,117.00
Rajasthan		3,73,649.02	3,73,649.02		1,15,395.02	1,15,395.02
Sikkim		24,955.00	24,955.00		7,707.00	7,707.00
Tamil Nadu	7,41,400.13	2,73,556.00	10,14,956.13	12,68,310.16	84,483.00	13,52,793.16
Telangana	1,65,711.00		1,65,711.00	51,177.00		51,177.00
Tripura		40,000.00	40,000.00		72,000.00	72,000.00
Uttar Pradesh			0.00		3,55,831.00	3,55,831.00
Uttarakhand		71,534.00	71,534.00		22,092.00	22,092.00
West Bengal		4,59,200.00	4,59,200.00		9,96,600.00	9,96,600.00
All States	25,12,738.13	38,49,160.02	64,20,062.16	42,21,746.36	24,94,907.33	67,58,876.90

Source: Budget documents of state governments (2018–19).

Notes

1. Press Information Bureau (PIB), press release dated 27 April 2018.
2. It is to be noted that along with rate cuts, GST rates for certain goods and services have also increased over the course of time.
3. It is only fair that many items of daily utility like detergents, shampoos, hair dyes, articles of cutlery and similar non-electronic domestic appliances, fans, sanitary ware, primary cells and batteries will now be charged at 18 per cent after this notification.
4. 'GST—Concept and Status' (2018), https://cbec-gst.gov.in/pdf/01052018-GST-Concept-Status.pdf (accessed 11 June 2018).
5. Minutes of 23rd GST Council Meeting held on 10 November 2017, Annexure 7—GST Return Filing (Experience & Suggestions), http://www.gstcouncil.gov.in/sites/default/files/Minutes/Signed%20Minutes%20-%2023rd%20GST%20Council%20Meeting.pdf (accessed 12 June 2018).
6. For instance, the deadline for GSTR-1, initially 31 December 2017, was extended to 10 January 2018. This benefitted both the monthly and the quarterly return filers filing returns for the period July–October 2017 and July–September 2017, respectively. Note that GSTR-1 has to be filed monthly if aggregate turnover is more than Rs 1.5 crore and quarterly if turnover is up to Rs 1.5 crore, in the preceding or current financial year.
7. In the same meeting, the decision with regard to the acquisition of the entire 51 per cent equity held by non-governmental institutions in GSTN, equally by the Centre and the state governments, was also taken. However, it remains to be seen whether this change in ownership will provide answers to the extant technical woes.
8. In addition, these businesses cannot carry out any interstate sales.
9. The IGST revenue is subject to apportionment and fund settlement between the Union and state governments, as a result of cross-utilisation of credits.
10. For this purpose, a projected nominal growth of 14 per cent per annum (base year 2015–16) is to be considered for revenue subsumed for a state.
11. In addition, cesses do not form part of the divisible pool of revenues shared with the states by the Union government, further increasing the vertical imbalance between the two tiers of the government.

12. The time period for such compensation has been stated in the Act as five years or for such period as may be prescribed on the recommendations of the GST Council.
13. Punjab published the SGST revenue for the month of July 2017 and has not updated the figures ever since.
14. These are, however, unaudited figures released by the respective state governments.
15. The state finance accounts do not give disaggregated revenue data for revenue collections from petroleum products, etc. (items that have been kept outside GST as of now).
16. PIB press release dated I June 2018.

Five

GST and the Informal Economy

Emerging Issues Post-GST in India

This chapter attempts to understand the nature and size of the informal economy in India. Furthermore, it tries to investigate the links between an informal economy and a broad-based indirect tax, and thereafter discusses the possible effects of GST on India's large informal sector and a huge section of the population that depends on it.

Globalisation has imposed an implicit barrier on setting an independent tax and expenditure policy. Increasing integration with the international market has placed national governments in a situation of strategic interaction with their counterparts elsewhere in setting the tax rate or designing a particular tax policy to attract private investment. Globalisation has also seen a homogenisation of tax policy and tax design. Countries have moved or are moving away from selective taxation (especially trade taxation) to broad-based consumption taxes. Consumption is primarily being taxed through the value-added tax (VAT). In the Indian case, the goods and services tax (GST) is the method of taxing the final consumption of goods and services at each stage of value added. The other methods of taxing consumption, like retail sales tax or turnover tax, have lost their relevance. This 'one size fits all' approach to tax policy is done when countries are different in terms of their economic structure, social sector outcome, public service delivery need and overall development. One of the major challenges in setting the tax policy in developing countries is the presence of a large informal sector. Since GST is a tax that operates through the method of tax credit, it is argued that with the introduction of GST, the informal sector will shrink.

This chapter will undertake a comparative understanding of GST and the informal economy. The key challenges for a particular tax design in developing countries as articulated by Keen (2007) are: (a) dealing with a large informal sector, and (b) determining the degree of reliance on trade taxes. With the pressure of globalisation, the reliance on trade taxes has declined steadily over the years.[1] Pressing revenue needs have thus made developing countries look for domestic revenue sources. Given the fact that the income tax base is narrow, the alternative source has been consumption tax. The most common tax imposed is VAT on consumption. As Keen (ibid.) points out, VAT has been adopted by more than 130 countries, including the poorest—for instance, around three quarters of all the countries in Sub-Saharan Africa now have a VAT. This has been and remains the centrepiece of tax reform in many developing countries.

As the nature of the informal economy is complex and differs across countries, one does not have a precise definition for it. The available estimates of the informal economy also vary widely across countries and are very sensitive to the methods of estimations. Apart from the definitional issue of what is informal, some common characteristics of the informal economy across the world are as follows:

(i) Low value added
(ii) High concentration of female labour force
(iii) Absence of regulations
(iv) Outside the purview of taxation
(v) Low wage rate, no job security and bad work conditions

The main objective of this chapter is to analyse the behaviour of the informal economy towards a particular tax design. In this case, we examine the impact of GST on the informal economy. The chapter also looks at whether the size of the informal economy changes with the change in the tax design with respect to the particular tax.

Background and Rationale

There has been no systematic study on the effect of taxation on the informal sector. While the problems and complexities involved in designing a tax system in a developing country are recognised in the tax literature at a theoretical level (Boadway et al. 2007; Emran and Stiglitz 2005; Gordon and Li 2009; Keen 2007; Munk and Sorensen 2004; Pigott and Whalley 2001), one is still not clear how a particular tax system affects production, distribution and various social outcomes. There is hardly any empirical understanding of how the informal sector gets affected by a particular taxation regime. At the theoretical level, there are contrasting views on this. Emran and Stiglitz (2005) argue that broad-based VAT may not be the appropriate tax; instead, international trade tax administered at the border may be more effective when there is a large informal sector. Keen (2008), on the other hand, argues that compared to the formal sector, the informal sector actually pays more taxes in the presence of GST as it is not able to get the benefits of tax credit available to the formal sector under a GST regime. Higher tax burden on the informal sector has the potential to reduce its size and eventually eliminate it from the economic system.

Research Question

As we know, the tax literature suggests that the introduction of GST will result in increasing formalisation of the economy since the input tax credit (ITC) method will make it difficult for the informal economy to survive under GST. The basic research question this chapter delves into is how the introduction of GST changes the structure of the economy and what effect it has on output and employment by looking at the experience of some states. The specific research objectives this chapter focuses on are as follows:

(a) An estimate of the informal economy, which is comparable across states as the nature of the informal economy differs across states.

(b) The nature of labour absorption in the informal economy, especially from a gender perspective.
(c) How the link between the formal economy and the informal economy operates in a given country context, taking into consideration key sectors under a particular tax regime.
(d) The structure of employment, value-added and other key ratios in the formal and informal sectors.
(e) Key tax policy changes like GST, its structure and design, and whether GST has resulted in changing the structure of formal and informal economies.

How Informal is the Indian Economy?

Estimating the size of the informal economy is a tedious task, given its opaque and discretionary nature. The National Sample Survey Office (NSSO) surveys are an extensive and reliable source of extracting data related to the informal economy.[2] Before any meaningful exercise to estimate the size of the informal economy, it is important to first clearly define the informal economy. The National Commission for Enterprises in the Unorganised Sector (NCEUS) provides clear definitions of the informal sector, informal employment and informal economy.

> Informal sector: [A]ll unincorporated private enterprises owned by individuals or households engaged in the sale and production of goods and services operated on a proprietary or partnership basis and with less than ten total workers. (NCEUS 2009: 1)
>
> Informal worker/employment: [T]hose working in the [informal] sector or households, excluding regular workers with social security benefits provided by the employers and [including] the workers in the formal sector without any employment and social security benefits provided by the employers. (ibid.: 3)
>
> Informal economy: The informal sector and its workers plus the informal workers in the formal sector constitute the informal economy. (ibid.)

What follows is a short discussion on the contribution of the informal economy to the labour market as well as national gross domestic product (GDP).

Informal Economy and Employment

Using the NCEUS definitions, the 2012 National Statistical Commission's *Report of the Committee on Unorganised Sector Statistics* (NSC 2012) presents estimates of the workforce employed in the formal and informal sectors of the Indian economy, which are reported in Tables 5.1 and 5.2. As is evident from the data, informality defines the Indian economy. Two broad findings emerge: First, it is the informal sector that absorbs roughly over four-fifths of workers. Second, within the formal sector also, more than half of the workers are informal workers, who are denied any employment or social security benefits by their employers. As a result, the size of the informal economy is a little more than 90 per cent of the total economy. It has been argued that any conservative estimate of the informal economy would also fail to convey the sheer size and magnitude of this sector that provides employment to a large segment of people. The contribution of this sector to the national GDP is also discussed in the subsequent section.

Table 5.1: Estimated Number of Informal/Formal Sector Workers: 1999–2000 (in million)

Worker		*Sector*		
		Informal	*Formal*	
	Informal	339.71 (99.5)	23.04 (42.0)	362.75 (91.5)
	Formal	1.79 (0.5)	31.85 (58.0)	33.64 (8.5)
		341.50 (86.15)	54.89 (13.85)	396.39

Source: NSC (2012).

Table 5.2: Estimated Number of Informal/Formal Sector Workers: 2004–05 (in million)

Worker		*Sector*		
		Informal	*Formal*	
	Informal	391.73 (99.6)	28.91 (46.2)	420.64 (92.3)
	Formal	1.42 (0.4)	33.65 (53.8)	35.07 (7.7)
		393.15 (86.27)	62.56 (13.73)	455.71

Source: NSC (2012).

A 2014 study by the Confederation of Indian Industry (CII) estimated the size and composition of employment in India for 2011–12 using unit-level data from the various NSSO rounds. Their analysis showed that while the share of the informal economy in the total economy was roughly the same—91.9 per cent—the share of informal-sector jobs reduced to 83 per cent (from roughly 86 per cent in 1999–2000 and 2004–05), which is a positive development. However, there are two worrying signs that emerge from the 2011–12 estimates: First, while total employment increased to 474.23 million in 2011–12, the rate of growth of total employment shrunk significantly, from around 15 per cent between 2004–05 and 1999–2000 to just 4 per cent between 2011–12 and 2004–05. Second, the share of informal jobs in the formal sector continued to rise—from 42 per cent in 1999–2000 to 54.6 per cent in 2011–12. So while the formal sector continues to gradually increase, it is employing more informal workers.

As a result, of the total 77.84 million new employment opportunities generated between 2011–12 and 1999–2000, 72.51 million jobs, i.e., 93 per cent of new employment opportunities, were informal in nature. Segregating this figure of 72.51 million conveys a stark reality—while 27.03 million jobs were created in the formal sector (34.7 per cent of total jobs), more than four-fifths of these jobs were informal, i.e., 21.7 million. Thus, it is seen that the drive towards formalisation is paradoxically increasing the space of the informal economy.

Given the enormity of the informal economy in India, it is thus evident that merely shrinking the size of the informal sector will be half the job done. Concerted efforts have to be exercised to formalise the nature of jobs and bring more employees under the social security net, which itself will shrink the size of the informal economy.

Informal Sector and Gross Value Added (GVA)

It is important to gauge the contribution of the informal sector to the national GDP. With respect to this contribution and its estimation, the NSC report (2012: 30) details the following.

> As per statistics available in India so far, it has been seen that GDP from unorganized sector is almost half of the total GDP. However, the very nature of this sector mostly characterized by the huge proliferation of tiny production units not or hardly maintaining any accounts and remaining invisible or non-observable in most of the times, does not allow direct measurement. In the Indian NAS [National Accounts Statistics] therefore, the estimates of GDP and also of GVA for unorganized sector by activity are compiled through indirect methods, using the benchmark indicator procedure.

The NSC report gives estimates of the total GVA by the informal sector, using NSSO data from the 54th and 61st rounds. These estimates suggest that the total GVA by the informal sector has increased by Rs 4,361,770 million between 1999–2000 and 2004–05 (a 44 per cent increase). The economic activities where the share of the informal sector in total GVA exceeds 50 per cent are presented in Table 5.3.

While there has been a decline in the share of the informal sector's contribution to total GVA for most economic activities, an

Table 5.3: Estimated Share of the Informal Sector in GAV by Economic Activities: 1999–2000 and 2004–05 (in per cent)

	1999–2000	*2004–05*
Agriculture	96.55	94.48
Trade	77.35	75.08
Hotels & Restaurants	56.19	50.80
Transport & Storage	57.27	44.45
Real Estate & Business Services	77.24	63.44
Commercial, Social & Personal Services	61.04	69.44
Private Households & Extra-Territorial Organisations	80.11	95.29

Source: NSC (2012).

increase is seen for construction; banking, finance and insurance; health and social work; commercial, social and personal services; and private households and extra-territorial organisations. However, for all economic activities combined, the share of the informal sector to total GVA has declined from 54.2 per cent in 1999–2000 to 49.94 per cent in 2004–05. The increase in the absolute contribution but the decrease in the share to total GVA by the informal sector during this period reflects the gradual increase in the formal sector, a positive development for the economy.

The latest estimates of the informal economy have been reported in the *Economic Survey of India 2017–18* (Ministry of Finance 2018). The *Economic Survey* (vol. 1) uses the following definition for capturing formality:

> First, when firms are providing some kind of social security to employees. In India, government provides this for its employees, and the Employees' Provident Fund Organization (EPFO) provides it to private sector employees in respect of pensions and provident funds; and the Employees' State Insurance Corporation (ESIC) in respect of medical benefits...A second definition of formality is when firms are part of the tax net. Since new data on the GST is available, one can define tax formality as firms having registered under the GST. (Ministry of Finance 2018: 40)

Using these definitions and data from various sources (GST registrations, EPFO/ESIC contributions, NSSO 68th and 73rd rounds), the *Economic Survey* estimates that of the total 71.29 million firms/enterprises, only 0.6 per cent of firms (0.4 million firms)—accounting for 38 per cent of the total turnover, 87 per cent of exports and 63 per cent of GST liability (average tax rate of 16.3 per cent)—constitute the formal sector (these firms belong both in the tax net and social security net). An additional 8.83 million firms are in the tax net—they are registered under GST, contribute 41 per cent to total turnover and 13 per cent to total exports and pay 37 per cent of tax liabilities (average tax rate of 7 per cent). However, these firms do not extend EPFP/ESIC benefits to their employees. On the other hand, there are 0.09 million firms that contribute 14 per cent to the total turnover—these are in the social security net but not in the tax net. Moreover, there are 61.98 million firms—86.93 per cent of total firms—that contribute only 6.9 per cent to the total turnover but are neither registered under the GST nor pay EPFO/ESIC. These are the purely informal firms that fall outside the tax net as well as the social security net.

How Will GST Impact the Informal Economy?

A recent World Bank Report (2018) points out that the Indian GST system is among the most complex in the world with not only one of the highest tax rates (of 28 per cent, which is the second highest among a sample of 115 countries that have a GST/VAT system and for which data is available) but also one of the largest number of tax slabs (four non-zero rates, which only five countries, including India, use). Needless to say, given this complex framework of the new tax regime, the structure of GST has attracted a lot of criticism from every quarter despite the obvious and much-anticipated benefits of this structural reform in Indian taxation. Thus, it is understandable that there is not much clarity among most stakeholders on the exact impact GST would have on the Indian economy. Additionally, given that it is a new tax and is constantly evolving to match the existing realities of the economy, any realistic estimation is a difficult exercise.

It is interesting to note that given the significant size of the informal economy in India, the academic discourse around the issue, though extremely insightful in laying forth the key issues, has been sketchy at best. One of the major reasons for this is that the inscrutable nature of the informal sector makes any scholarship in this sector of the economy a painstaking exercise. In this context, a discussion on the anticipated impact of GST on the informal economy is pertinent. Towards this end, a brief review of such discussions, along with a study on the anticipated impact of GST on the informal economy, is presented next (the discussions are often blurred on the distinction between informal sector and informal economy).

GST and the Informal Economy/Sector: Likely Gains

The most laudable achievement of GST is its potential to formalise the economy, which, in turn, has many advantages. The biggest challenge regarding the informal sector has been its concealing veil that misses the government's regulatory sight as well as escapes all prevailing labour regulations. GST is seen as an instrument to achieve forced formalisation—informal firms will be forced to join the GST network to preserve their market share. Their inability or unwillingness to join the network would essentially mean that the formal-sector firms in the vertical supply chain would shift to those formal firms that can raise GST-compliant tax invoices and facilitate the ITC mechanism. Thus, it is believed that this in-built mechanism to comply is the biggest strength of GST that will aid formalisation.

While some have argued that this forced formalisation would be at the cost of the informal sector that employs a large proportion of the workforce, Prabhat Patnaik (2017) has rightly pointed out that:

> If the process of primitive accumulation-cum-centralisation in the 'informal' sector occurs as a consequence of the expansion of the 'formal' sector, i.e. as an accompaniment of a process of accumulation of capital in the latter, then the destruction of the 'informal' sector, though tragic in itself, provides nonetheless a buoyancy to the 'formal' sector.

With increased formalisation, the informal firms' labour force would have access to better working conditions, which would include, among other benefits, access to legal rights and redress mechanisms, as well as social security benefits. It has also been stated that access to credit from financial institutions would be an advantage of formalisation since it 'not only helps avoid usurious informal lenders but also provides a platform for capitalization of assets in order to mobilize resources' (PFPAC 2017).

The expected reduction in the size of the informal sector will be to great advantage to especially those sectors that at present have a high proportion of unorganised firms. A study reported that sectors such as apparel, tiles and sanitary ware, plywood, textile, footwear, electrical equipment and appliances, and plastics and packaging have a high composition of unorganised firms. It further states that

> analysts expect the share of the informal segment in the tiles industry to decline from 40% currently to 20%. Similarly, nearly 60% of the ready-mixed concrete market is unorganized. In the light electrical segment, more than 35% of the businesses are in the informal sector. Certainly, this augurs well for larger companies in the organized sector. This also comes at a time when volume growth has just recovered from the effects of demonetisation and corporate India is desperate for a much-awaited earnings recovery. (*Livemint* 2017)

Thus, it is evident that the GST rollout promises formalisation of the economy, with manifold benefits. However, the materialisation of formalisation as envisaged is a farfetched expectation. The structural transition to GST is not without impediments, many of which are specifically adverse to the informal sector and informal economy.

GST and the Informal Economy/Sector: Potential Challenges

One of the biggest challenges for the informal sector is going to be the burden of operating costs, which are bound to go up as firms have to hire accountants and computerise their operations to file GST returns.[3] The 37 mandatory annual filings (three a month plus an annual return) for each state the firm operates in is going to place a heavy cost, both in terms of time and money, especially on the smaller firms, a vast proportion of which lack the institutional arrangement to comply with GST requirements. And since these costs are in a sense fixed in nature, they would entail a higher burden on the smaller firms than the large ones, which would in turn undermine the viability of the former.

The GST procedural rigours are often cited as the biggest impediment to any meaningful transition of the taxation regime. T. N. Ninan (2017) reports that

> Between 25 and 30 per cent of the seven-plus million businesses that have migrated to the GST system have not been filing their returns. About 40 per cent of those who have been filing report zero returns. Also, 95 per cent of those filing to report tax paid have an average payment of perhaps not more than Rs. 20,000.

These figures are an indication of the poor filing compliance by millions of businesses and if such a scenario continues to persist, then poor compliance will defeat any meaningful attempt to match tax invoices, which, in effect, shall render the implementation of GST futile. Thus, a fundamental change in making the filing of GST returns simpler and user-friendly, along with providing the adequate infrastructural support, are the needs of the hour. Otherwise it is hard to imagine how the government aims to bring the 61.98 million informal firms/enterprises into the GST tax net.

If indeed these informal firms were successfully brought under the tax net, the burden of tax would eat into their profit margins and further undermine their viability. This is because the coverage of the GST regime to include the informal firms would amount to a redistribution of the tax burden from the 'formal' to the 'informal' sector, if GST were assumed to be revenue neutral. This, according to Prabhat Patnaik (2017), would lead 'to a process of primitive accumulation-cum-centralisation of capital' in the formal sector. Needless to say, this too shall come with its own challenges. Also, it may be noted that while defending the informal firms on grounds of tax avoidance is not justifiable, a conducive environment needs to be provided to the informal firms to ensure they have a smooth transition to GST that does not eat into their profit right away and marginalise them to a state where their viable existence is threatened.

Another major concern that has been voiced is the impact of GST on employment. If the transition of the informal sector to the formal sector is indeed materialised, whether or not there shall be a proportionate absorption by the formal sector of the vast labour force employed in the informal sector remains an area of concern. It is of paramount importance that the government lay out a clear blueprint on the likely employment scenario in the country post-GST and put similar efforts into outlining how the transition of employees from the informal to the formal sector shall materialise alongside the envisaged transition of firms from the informal to a formal set-up. Given that such a transition shall entail a large fiscal cost (to cover employees' social security benefits), the lack of reflection of the government on this issue is a disturbing sign and poses a precarious risk to the overall macroeconomic environment of the country.

An accompanying concern related to the anticipated job squeeze in the informal sector (without a commensurate increase in jobs in the formal sector) is its likely impact on demand. Prabhat Patnaik (2017) succinctly presents this alternative scenario:

> But if the reduction in the 'informal' sector is not part of such a process but is an ex cathedra action imposed by the State from

> above, then this reduction, far from stimulating any accompanying expansion in the 'formal' sector, reduces, on the contrary, the level of activity in the latter through its multiplier effects. The activity in the 'formal' sector, after all, is sustained in part by demand from the 'informal' sector itself, and if the latter shrinks for independent reasons, having nothing to do with the former's expansion, then the former too cannot escape some reduction. The entire economy consequently gets caught in a downturn in activity.

Many have argued that this could very well be a possibility, especially having witnessed the after-shocks of the demonetisation drive that, apart from hitting the informal sector the hardest, choked demand and adversely impacted growth. Arun Kumar also argues that the unorganised sector is not prepared to cope with the complicated GST and that the GST impact, superimposed on the impact of demonetisation, is detrimental to the informal sector. Questioning the rationale of this tax on these small informal firms, he states that 'One nation, one tax is very good for the large scale industries, but for the small business dealings, it is local purchase and local sale' (*The Economic Times* 2017b).

Even though it is a difficult task to disentangle the individual effects of demonetisation and GST, it is clear that the lack of clarity on the likely impact of these measures on the informal sector have hurt this sector dearly. The United Nations Conference on Trade and Development's (UNCTAD) 2017 report stated that the output of the informal sector has contracted because of the twin blows of demonetisation and GST. 'The decline in the output of the informal sector when it is properly measured will show even a sharper decline in the GDP growth than the 5.7 per cent recorded in the April–June quarter of 2017–18.'[4] While many perceive these after-effects to be transitory in nature and as part of the 'teething trouble' associated with the birth of a new regime, not all concerns are unfounded. The red flags raised need to be revisited in order to ensure that the economy can reap the benefits of the GST regime.

Notes

1. Although it has a significant share in revenues.
2. NSSO uses the terms 'informal' and 'unorganised' interchangeably.
3. Some have argued that this negative impact may be smaller than expected as most of the informal firms/enterprises would continue to operate outside the GST framework (most have a turnover less than the GST threshold, and some may avail the flat-rate payment). However, the argument seems to be a red herring—the proponents of this argument have missed the crucial fact that operating outside the GST framework would in fact result in the marginalisation of these informal enterprises due to their unsuitability to raise tax invoices.
4. https://www.orfonline.org/expert-speak/the-shocked-informal-sector/ (accessed 20 January 2018).

Six

One Nation, One Tax

'One nation, one tax' and a common market underpin the rationale of implementing the goods and services tax (GST) in India. The electronic way bill or e-way bill was supposed to pave the way for a common market with its ability to facilitate the seamless movement of goods within the country. Logistical glitches like complex paperwork and time delays at interstate checkposts have often been posited as reasons that impede the efficient transportation of goods within the country. Also, the different rules in different states regarding the movement of goods (under the value-added tax [VAT] regime) made the clearance processes for buyers, sellers and transporters cumbersome. At the same time, these led to slip-ups in the efficient tracking of transported goods. A single e-way bill was expected to root out such transit delays and, at the same time, help plug tax evasion by having a uniform provision for the movement of goods in the country. This, according to a report in *The Hindu Business Line* (2018), will reap far-reaching benefits:

> Logistical speed-breakers cost the Indian economy an extra $45 billion or 4.3 per cent of GDP every year, a McKinsey report says. Therefore, any change in the system that brings about even small benefits is to be welcomed. If you are a retail investor in the shares of manufacturing companies, remember, seamless shipments perk profits and returns. The LPI Survey by World Bank in 2014 put logistics costs at 14 per cent of the total value of goods in India, while it is only 6–8 per cent in other major countries. The GST E-way bill combination was expected to trim logistics costs by 20 per cent.

In this light, this chapter discusses the various aspects of the e-way bill, including its current status.

What is an E-Way Bill?

An e-way bill is a receipt or a document issued by a carrier, giving details and instructions relating to the shipment of a consignment of goods, and the details include the names of consignor and consignee, the point of origin of the consignment, its destination and its route. It is basically a compliance mechanism wherein by way of a digital interface, the person causing the movement of goods worth more than Rs 50,000 has to upload the relevant information (details of the goods, their consignor, recipient and transporter) prior to the commencement of movement and generate an e-way bill on the GST portal. The GST laws provide flexibility in allowing any of the parties to a transaction—the consignor, the recipient or the transporter—to generate the e-way bill, provided they are registered.

Rule 138 of the Central Goods and Services Tax (CGST) Rules, 2017 provides for the e-way bill mechanism. In this context, it is important to note that 'information is to be furnished prior to the commencement of movement of goods' and that the bill 'is to be issued whether the movement is in relation to a supply or for reasons other than supply'.[1]

Thus, by providing a digital interface that facilitates faster movement of goods, an e-way bill is bound to improve the turnaround time of vehicles and help the logistics industry by increasing the average distances travelled, reducing the travel time as well as costs. Additionally, other than the list of exempted goods as stated in Rule 138 of the CGST Rules, 2017, the e-way bill thus lays the groundwork for a system where movement of goods worth over Rs 50,000 shall not fall outside the regulatory sight of the government. As a result, it promises efficient tracking of goods moving within the country, and thus an in-built mechanism to close channels for potential tax evasion on this account.

Where We Stand Today on the E-Way Bill

The 22nd GST Council Meeting held on 6 October 2017 decided to roll out the e-way bill system from 1 January 2018 in a staggered manner in the states and to implement it across the country from 1 April 2018. However, its implementation was delayed mainly on two accounts—the lack of states' preparedness to implement it and the delay in getting the requisite technical infrastructure in place.

Yet again, a sound digital interface that works flawlessly to facilitate timely and user-friendly uploading of e-way bills along with ensuring that errors and mismatches are rooted out is a prerequisite to reaping any of the envisaged benefits associated with e-way bills. Unlike GST returns, e-way bills have to be uploaded in real time. Hence, the success of e-way bills in GST is contingent upon a robust technical infrastructure that forms the backbone of GST. However, it is interesting to note that the technical preparedness has fallen short of expectations and this has inadvertently caused delays in implementation of e-way bills. While different states have different opinions regarding the appropriate date for implementation of the same, given their extant information technology (IT) infrastructure, even the National Informatics Centre (NIC) has been unable to put the requisite infrastructure in place.

In the 24th GST Council Meeting held on 16 December 2017, it was flagged that the delay in procuring the software licence by the NIC was one of the reasons for the delay. Additionally, the NIC suggested a staggered approach for implementing e-way bills for both interstate and intra-state movement of goods to avoid the early technical glitches associated with the filing of GST returns in the initial days. The chairman of the Goods and Services Tax Network (GSTN) stated that

> if a choice was given to the States regarding the date for introduction of e-Way Bill System for intra-State movement of goods and if all States decided to implement it from an earlier

> date, then the system of NIC might not be able to take the load as full testing had not been done till date.[2]

He further added that 'according to their [GSTN] estimates, a total of about 30 lakh e-Way bills were likely to be generated daily for both inter-State and intra-State movement of goods and in the absence of full testing of software, it was desirable to have a phased implementation.'[3]

With respect to the preparedness of various states in the country, it is to be noted that while most states are geared to implement the e-way bill system for interstate movement of goods, most states do not have the requisite infrastructure to implement e-way bills for intra-state movement of goods. In the 24th GST Council Meeting held on 16 December 2017, states expressed their concerns regarding the same, and the secretary of the council stated that '14 States did not have any e-Way Bill System and the taxpayers and the transporters in these States would find it difficult to implement the e-Way Bill System.' As for the states that had the required provisions, he stated that 'the States already having e-Way Bill System could use the enabling provision and continue to use the same until the Central server and the software were fully ready'.[4] Some other concerns and suggestions shared by representatives from the states included loss in revenue on account of the delay in the implementation of the e-way bill system, taking steps to ensure that taxpayers cannot subvert the system by splitting the consignment value to less than Rs 50,000, bringing gold under the provision of the system to stop the movement of smuggled gold (this was raised by the representative from Kerala, and the same was countered by the representative from Bihar), and revisiting the validity period of e-way bills. Accommodating all the states' concerns as well as suggestions of the GSTN, the council approved that (i) the nationwide e-way bill system for interstate movement of goods be introduced on a trial basis latest by 16 January 2018 and on a compulsory basis with effect from 1 February 2018, and (ii) states may choose any date before 1 June 2018 for implementing the national e-way bill system for intra-state movement of goods, but all states shall implement it by 1 June 2018.

As a result, it was only after eight months of the GST being rolled out on 1 July 2017 that we had a nationwide e-way bill implemented for the interstate movement of goods. While the e-way bill for interstate movement of goods came into force with effect from 1 April 2018, the timeline for implementation of this e-way bill was extended till June 2018 (states could do it in a staggered manner and choose any date on or before 1 June 2018). However, vide a press release dated 10 April 2018, it was announced that the e-way bill system for intra-state movement of goods would be implemented from 15 April 2018 in Andhra Pradesh, Gujarat, Kerala, Telangana and Uttar Pradesh. In fact, it is already in force in Karnataka with effect from 1 April 2018.[5] It is important to gather experiences from all the states to assess the effectiveness of e-way bills in ensuring the seamless movement of goods in the country as well as compliance to the tax rules.

Notes

1. http://cbec.gov.in/resources//htdocs-cbec/gst/E%20Way%20Bill%20Provisions%20in%20GST_Web.pdf;jsessionid=076D796E73CE1EE71274D3562AE48B70 (accessed 14 March 2018).
2. Minutes of Meeting, 24th GST Council Meeting, http://gstcouncil.gov.in/sites/default/files/Minutes/Signed%20Minutes%20-%2024th%20GST%20Council%20Meeting.pdf (accessed 20 March 2018).
3. Ibid.
4. Ibid.
5. PIB Press Release, dated 10 April 2018.

Seven

Feasibility of a Common Market

The goods and services tax (GST) in India was promulgated with the phrase 'one nation, one tax, one market'. It is important to note that while the notion of 'one tax' clearly falls flat (given the multiple rate structures that we have) and has been analysed at length, little has been discussed around the idea of 'one market'. However, to be fair, the idea of 'one tax' is not in conflict with multiple tax rates. It is a different story that the Indian GST design has taken the multiple rate structure a bit too far. This has resulted in complications in implementing the tax as well as in compliance. As our analysis shows, there are global experiences where a uniform GST has been successfully implemented with more than one rate of GST. Since GST as a concept is uniform across the country, the question is: Can this GST design help develop a common market for India?

The GST has been said to pave the way for a common market that will be facilitated by the seamless movement of goods and services across the states of India. Before we discuss the impediments to the free movement of goods and services across states in the pre- and post-GST eras, it is important to understand what a common market means. The idea of a common market is usually associated with that of Europe. It is traced to the treaty signed by six European nations in 1957 that aimed at gradually eliminating trade barriers between those member nations. The idea of a common market developed over time to facilitate economic integration among member nations by providing a free trade area with no tariffs for goods and relatively free movement of capital and services. However, certain non-tariff barriers like standard regulatory requirements impeded full integration. A single market requires complete access to four freedoms—movement of goods, capital, services and people. The European Union today stands as a classic example of having a single market that has opened up markets between member nations and helped in economic prosperity by eliminating internal borders and/or other regulatory obstacles.

The European model has paved the way for the development of the Eurasian Economic Union, the single-market Eurasian Economic Space (EEC) or Single Economic Space, providing a foundation for the same. Initially consisting of Belarus, Kazakhstan and Russia, the EEC was enlarged to include Armenia and Kyrgyzstan in 2015 to provide a fillip to economic growth among these six nations. Similarly, the common market in the East African Community (EAC) aims to accelerate economic growth and development among the EAC partner nations. It is interesting to note that along with the four freedoms, these nations have two additional rights, namely right of establishment and right of residence, which have further strengthened economic integration between member nations.

If we shift gears to India now, two fundamental questions need to be answered. One, does GST explicitly define the notion of a common/single market? Two, is the concept of a common market that was floated with the rollout of GST in India similar to the internationally prevalent one, as discussed earlier? With respect to the first question, it is to be noted that there is no explicit mention of the conditions that shall lay the preconditions for the formation of a common market with the implementation of GST in India. This is in stark contrast to the international experience, where the freedoms to be made accessible to member nations under the ambit of a common/single market have been clearly elucidated. While answering the second question, we observe that the understanding of a common/single market has gained traction in the international context where complete free movement of goods, services, capital and people has been attempted without regard to the national boundaries of member nations. The Indian common market idea, however, has a unique take on this ubiquitous idea, where GST is supposed to eliminate the extant trade barriers not among some member nations, but across the provinces of the same country. Thus, the common market under GST is a domestic one, which aims to render state boundaries ineffective in impeding the seamless movement of goods. To understand how this anticipated common market shall materialise, we need to understand the taxation system pre and post-GST.

In this context, it may first be noted that unlike her international counterparts, the creation of a common market in India requires only the freedom of free movement of goods from one state of the country to another. The other three freedoms to be made accessible for the creation of a common market—freedom of movement of people,[1] capital and services—are already guaranteed under the Indian Constitution. Even with respect to the freedom of goods, Article 301 of the Indian Constitution states that 'subject to the other provisions (302–307) of this Part (Part XII), trade, commerce and intercourse throughout the territory of India shall be free.' One such provision is stated in Article 302: 'Parliament may by law impose such restrictions on the freedom of trade, commerce or intercourse between one State and another or within any part of the territory of India as may be required in the public interest.' The intent behind Article 301 was to break down barriers between states to create an economic unit for national advantage, but the introduction of a tax was imminent in light of the need for the Union to coordinate the whole sphere of interstate sales. Thus, the central sales tax (CST) was levied on interstate trade or commerce. The CST Act, 1956 was enacted

> to formulate principles for determining when a sale or purchase of goods takes place in the course of inter-state trade or commerce or outside the State or in the course of import into or export from India, to provide for the levy, collection and distribution of taxes on sales of goods in the course of inter-State trade or commerce and to declare certain goods to be of special importance in inter-State trade or commerce and specify the restrictions and conditions to which State laws imposing taxes on the sale or purchase of such goods of special importance shall be subject.[2]

The act stated that though CST is a central levy, it is to be administered by the concerned state in which the sale originates and the entire revenue accruing under levy of CST is to be collected and kept by the state in which the sale originates. The initial idea was to track the movement of goods crossing state borders and minimise evasion of taxes on this account. However, with time, the structure of CST attracted criticism. One, the CST rate was gradually increased from 1 per cent to 2 per cent, then to 3 per cent and, with effect from 1 July 1975, to 4 per cent. Introduced as an instrument with a regulatory overreach of the taxman on sales that are affected in the course of interstate trade, it became a source for state governments to mobilise tax revenue and strengthen their fiscal positions. However, being an origin-based tax, CST was inconsistent with the principles of value-added tax (VAT), which is a destination-based tax with an inherent input tax credit refund. The CST rate was reduced from 3 per cent to 2 per cent with effect from 1 June 2008. While the reduction of the CST rate, first from 4 per cent to 3 per cent in 2007, and then to 2 per cent in 2008 was a step in the right direction, it still impeded the seamless movement of goods across states by having a skewed structure that benefited the origin-state at the expense of the importing state.

Currently, GST has subsumed CST, and the former, being a destination-based tax, is expected to restore the imbalance between the importing and exporting states that prevailed until now. However, whether this alone guarantees the creation of a common market will demand further enquiry. First, it is pertinent to realise that while CST has been done away with, a plethora of local entry taxes remain that will continue to constrain the seamless movement of goods across states. While the magnitude of economic costs that these local taxes entail may be small, until and unless these local taxes are subsumed under GST in theory and practice, they will impede the creation of a common market. Second, infrastructural impediments need to be minimised to facilitate the smooth movement of goods and services across states that can foster a common market. Prior to the introduction of GST, checkposts and the complex tax structure impeded the seamless movement of goods across state borders and contributed inadvertently to delays as well as higher logistical costs.[3] However, a unified tax regime obviates the need for these checkposts and is expected to facilitate efficient interstate movement of goods. Thus, with the rollout of GST on 1 July 2017, as many as 22 states and Union Territories abolished their checkposts, while the rest were in the process of doing so.[4] Instead, the integrated goods and services tax (IGST) is what shall provide the bedrock for smooth assessment and accounting of interstate trade. The e-way bill system has a crucial role to play to facilitate this, and it was noted that the initial delay in the implementation of nationwide e-way bills for interstate trade had led to severe revenue leakages.

In the 24th GST Council Meeting held on 16 December 2017, some states expressed concerns over the delay in the nationwide implementation of the e-way bill system. Kerala reported that approximately 80 per cent of consumer goods came from other states without IGST payment, which hurt state revenues. Bihar also reported reduced import into the state to the tune of about Rs 10,000 crore during July–October 2017 due to the e-way bill system not being enforced in time. The lack of information technology (IT) preparedness was also cited as one of the reasons for the delay in implementation of the same. Finally, the operations of the e-way bill system started on 1 April 2018, and it is expected to facilitate smooth movement of goods across state borders, thus being a step towards the creation of a common market. However, a robust technical infrastructure will be critical to sustain any attempt at creating a common market. Thus, it is evident that while the initial groundwork has been laid, the GST has to evolve over time to address these concerns for the creation of a common market.

As per the 2016–17 budget estimate (BE), India's tax to gross domestic product (GDP) ratio, taking the Union and states together, is 17.80 per cent. In this, the Union government's ratio is 10.83 per cent, whereas the states' ratio is 6.99 per cent of GDP. The combined indirect tax to GDP ratio for the country is 12.10 per cent, in which the Union's ratio is 5.25 per cent and the states' share is 6.84 per cent of GDP. For the states, inflows from taxes subsumed under GST formed the principal source of revenue. The direct tax share in the total collection of states is insignificant. Given the magnitude of the revenue, the country as a whole has no option but to have a positive GST impact on the revenue of governments at the Centre and the state levels. This is crucial to finance the much-needed expenditure at both levels of government.

Notes

1. Article 19 of the Indian Constitution guarantees citizens freedom of movement across states of India (certain exceptions being Scheduled Tribes areas and army areas).
2. http://wbcomtax.nic.in/Act_Rule_Schedule_Form/CST_Act.pdf (accessed 17 January 2018).
3. Monitoring and collection of sales tax at interstate checkposts caused much of the delay. Congestion at these points leads to slow movement of freight and passengers, and eventually higher costs and more pollution. While an average truck in India covered just 50,000–60,000 km a year, a truck in the US could cover 3 lakh km on average. Moreover, the cost of logistics as a percentage of the total value of goods is around 14 per cent in India, as against 6–8 per cent in other major countries (Ministry of Road Transport & Highways Press Release, 26 July 2017, Press Information Bureau).
4. Ministry of Finance Press Release, 3 July 2017, Press Information Bureau.

Eight

Evaluating Indian GST in Light of International Experience

Introduction

As emphasised earlier, goods and services tax (GST) has spread aggressively throughout the world and has been adopted by many countries. Every country has moulded the basic GST structure taking into account its unique economic, demographic and political context. India has learned from the experiences of different countries. Yet, it had to wait for almost eight years till GST was first announced in April 2010. Numerous rounds of tough negotiations have led us to where we are. However, it is noteworthy that this is just the beginning of a long journey. GST should essentially be viewed as a marathon and not a 100-metre dash.[1]

The initial few months after the GST launch were full of turmoil, with frequent changes in rules and numerous deadline extensions. However, almost a year and a half after the debut of GST, and with stability in the core GST structure, a comparison of the key design features of GST in India with experiences from the rest of the world is possible. Across countries, GST differs on a number of features. Some of the most important features are discussed in this chapter.

Tax Rates

The number of tax rates and exemptions are the most crucial part of a tax regime. There is almost universal acceptance on having only one rate (this essentially means two rates, as exports should be zero-rated) without any exemption (Bird and Gendron 2007: 108). This is because with multiple rates and exemptions, the central purpose of a GST—increased efficiency in tax administration emanating from a simple tax regime—is compromised. Administratively, more rates seem to be associated with high administrative and compliance costs (Cnossen 2004). However, seldom do countries heed this advice, and this is true for developed and developing countries alike. For example, Switzerland has slab rates of 2.5 per cent and 3.7 per cent, other than the standard rate of 7.7 per cent.[2]

Even countries known to have a uniform VAT rate may in fact have multiple rates. New Zealand, for example, put into effect a standard GST rate of 15 per cent from 1 October 2010, but on a closer look, it becomes evident that some services are taxed at an effective rate of 9 per cent. Moreover, real estate transactions and supply of precious metals, among others, are exempt from GST in New Zealand (EY 2018). Another example is Jamaica, which had a standard rate of 15 per cent in 2004. But among other variations, it imposed a rate of 12.5 per cent on some construction inputs and rates varying from 0 per cent to 157 per cent on motor vehicles (Bird and Gendron 2007: 109).

Singapore, however, is an example of a single-rate VAT with minimum exemptions. It introduced a VAT (called GST) of 3 per cent in April 1994, which was subsequently increased to 7 per cent in three separate hikes (Zhou et al. 2013).[3] This rate is one of the lowest in the Asia-Pacific region. Furthermore, exemptions are only limited to residential property, precious metals and financial transactions. However, as Singapore grapples with an ageing population and increased health and public support expenditure, it has been proposed that the tax rate be increased to 9 per cent by 2025 to boost government revenue.[4]

There are various reasons for countries opting for multiple rates, including zero-rating on goods other than exports, rather than a single uniform rate with no exemptions.[5] One of them is equity consideration. Taxing essentials for the poor, like food items, is likely to increase their price (Ahmad and Stern 1988). It should be noted that the rich would appropriate most of the benefits (in absolute terms) of such zero-rating, since they consume more of the exempted goods in absolute terms (International Tax Dialogue 2005). Still, in the wake of the relatively heavy burden of such taxes on the poor and in the absence of any other offsetting mechanism from the government, such a relief measure is justifiable (Bird and Gendron 2007: 77). Countries around the world have either zero-rated or exempted many goods and services that are essential for the poor. South Africa zero rates, among other goods, paraffin, an illuminating fuel widely used by the poor. Similarly, Canada zero rates basic food and prescription drugs, while exempting healthcare and education, among others (ibid.: 126; EY 2018).

As mentioned earlier, other than the 0 per cent and standard rate of 18 per cent, India has tax rates of 5 per cent, 12 per cent and 28 per cent for different classes of goods. Moreover, there is a special 3 per cent GST for gold. There is some complexity around zero rating and exemptions as well. The GST law differentiates between nil-rated, zero-rated, exempted and non-taxable supplies. Zero-rated supplies comprise exports and supplies to Special Economic Zone (SEZ) developers or units. For such goods, input tax credit can be claimed. For nil-rated supplies, 0 per cent tax is applicable, but input tax credit is not available. The most necessary food items feature in this category. Non-taxable supply of goods and services are those on which tax is not charged under the Central Goods and Services Tax (CGST) Act, but they are taxable under some other legislation. Examples of non-taxable goods include alcohol for human consumption, petroleum products and electricity. Exempted supplies is a broad term that includes nil-rated supplies, non-taxable supplies and the supplies notified under section 11 of the CGST Act. No input credit is allowed for exempted supplies.[6]

Having so many rates is always frowned upon, but the Indian situation can also be explained through the equity argument. Nil rating (and not zero rating) mostly applies to food items, whereas the 28 per cent rate applies mostly to luxury and sin goods. This has been done considering the stark inequalities that India faces today. A standard rate in lieu of different rates would have been sound economics. In the process of expanding the tax base, the prices of essential commodities would have increased, hitting the poor very hard. Further, a tax rate charged alike on subsistence goods and affluence goods can prove to be highly regressive and politically not feasible. The government is aware of such a state of affairs and has categorically shot down the calls for a single GST rate. Prime Minister Narendra Modi has stated, 'It would have been very simple to have just one slab but it would have meant we could not have food items at zero per cent tax rate. Can we have milk and Mercedes at the same rate?'[7]

However, this is not to say that there is no scope for unifying the tax rates in India. In the wake of GST revenues consistently rising and filling up its coffers, the government has hinted at bringing down the number of items in the highest tax slab of 28 per cent (it has already been brought down to 50 items from 200). Representatives of the government have also regularly reiterated that rationalisation of tax rates is on their agenda.[8] Eventually, the 28 per cent slab should make way for a broader base 18 per cent standard tax rate.

Nevertheless, the reasons for some exemptions, zero rating or lower taxation are not always clear, which certainly cannot be justified on equity grounds. Jordan, for example, zero rates printing services for any party, whereas The Netherlands (among many other countries) exempts betting and gambling from VAT (EY 2018). India's 3 per cent tax rate on gold also falls in the same category. It is clear that in many countries, forces other than just consideration for the poor are also often at work.

Registration Threshold and Compliance Costs

Another key feature is the threshold set for compulsory registration under the tax regime. Most governments switching over to a GST do so to increase their revenue flows. Thus, the most logical way forward seems to be to tax all transactions possible, that is, widening the registrant base to the highest workable limit under the tax system. And indeed, countries like Belgium, Chile, Mexico and The Netherlands do not have any registration threshold, i.e., any individual or business carrying out a taxable activity should be registered with the tax authorities (Annacondia and van der Corput 2003; OECD 2003, 2004a, 2004b, 2006). This argument, however, assumes that the administrative and compliance costs are zero, which is never true. One of the major arguments for VAT acceptability across countries is that it will reduce administrative and compliance costs.

However, with growing wisdom from evidence from various countries, experts have started favouring a more reasonable registration threshold. The world over, the majority of the VAT revenue is made up by a few large taxpayers. Keen and Mintz (2004) note that it is worthwhile to free up the administrative effort from numerous low-return taxpayers and spend more time and energy on medium and large taxpayers. Other than bringing higher revenue, it also brings efficiency in the administration and reduces compliance costs for small and marginal firms. It is, therefore, noteworthy that a majority of the countries with some form of VAT have a threshold that is well above zero. Some extreme examples for such a threshold are Singapore and the United Kingdom (UK). While Singapore has a threshold of almost USD 7,32,000, the UK has an even higher threshold of almost USD 1,12,000 (converted by the author using 4 July 2018 rates). Table 8.1 provides the threshold levels in various countries, expressed in their local currencies as well as in USD.

Table 8.1: VAT Thresholds in Selected Countries

Country	*Threshold (Local Currency)*	*Threshold (USD)*
Australia	75,000 AUD	55,400
Belgium	0	0
Brazil	0	0
Canada	CAD 30,000	22,800

(*Contd*)

(*Table 8.1 contd*)

Country	*Threshold (Local Currency)*	*Threshold (USD)*
China	Monthly turnover of CNY 5,000–20,000 for goods and services or Daily turnover of CNY 300–500	750–3,000 or 45–75
Croatia	HRK 3,00,000	47,000
Egypt	EGP 500,000	27,900
Germany	0	0
India	INR 20,00,000 INR 10,00,000 (for special category states)	29,000
Italy	0	0
Japan	JPY 10 million	90,400
Jordan	Goods (Trade): JOD 75,000 Services: JOD 30,000 Manufacturing: JOD 50,000	1,05,700 42,200 70,400
Mexico	0	0
The Netherlands	0	0
New Zealand	NZD 60,000	40,500
Russia	0	0
Singapore	SGD 1,00,000	7,32,000
South Africa	ZAR 1,00,000	72,900
Turkey	0	0
United Kingdom	GBP 85,000	1,12,000

Note: AUD—Australia Dollar; CAD—Canada Dollar; CNY—China Yuan/Renminbi; HRK—Croatia Kuna; EGP—Egypt Pound; INR—India Rupee; JPY—Japan Yen; JOD—Jordan Dinar; NZD—New Zealand Dollar; SGD—Singapore Dollar; ZAR—South Africa Rand; GBP—Great Britain Pound.

Source: EY (2018); conversion by author's own calculations using 4 July 2018 exchange rates.

The practice of changing thresholds should also be performed carefully. There have been instances, like in Egypt, where the threshold was reduced to zero without a commensurate increase in the tax administration's capacity. This decreases the effort spent for larger taxpayers (Bird and Gendron 2007: 119) and is expected to unnecessarily overburden the tax administration.

Another feature closely related to not only the threshold limit but also administrative efficiency is the extent to which the informal sector is taxed. One of the reasons cited for the introduction of GST is bringing the informal sector under the tax net. The informal sector consists mainly of small business enterprises unregistered with the tax authorities and is often called the shadow economy. But attempting to bring such enterprises under the tax net can sometimes do more harm than good. A VAT system can prove to be complex and, depending on its implementation, quite cumbersome. This imposes a significant compliance cost on small businesses. A study done for Croatia (Blazic 2004) found that VAT compliance costs formed around 31 per cent of the total revenues of businesses with fewer than six employees. Studies done for the UK and New Zealand have also noted significant compliance costs for businesses, especially small ones (Sandford 2000; Sandford and Hasseldine 1992). A negative correlation between compliance costs and firm size is observed as well. This makes the GST compliance costs highly regressive, i.e., the costs are relatively higher for smaller firms (Dickinson and White 2008). Forcing such costs on small and marginal businesses can prove to be disastrous, especially in middle- and lower-income countries, where these industries are the major source of employment for a large number of unskilled labour. One obvious way to minimise the effect of such compliance costs on the economy is to maintain reasonable registration thresholds and regularly update them.

The Indian threshold for registration is Rs 20,00,000, i.e., a person or a business with an annual turnover of less than Rs 20,00,000 is exempted from registration. For north-eastern and hilly states, this limit has been set at Rs 10,00,000.

In the pre-GST era, taxpayers with an annual turnover of more than Rs 1 crore accounted for almost 95 per cent of the sales turnover in India. As is clear from Table 8.2, taxpayers having a turnover of 0–25 lakh constituted just 0.90 per cent of the total turnover, and the 0–1 crore band accounted for just 3.34 per cent of the total turnover. The committee set up to ascertain the revenue neutral rate (RNR) suggested a registration threshold of Rs 40 lakh (Ministry of Finance 2015).[9] It is evident that like the rest of the world, India also derives most of its indirect tax revenue from only a few big taxpayers. Therefore, a strong case for keeping the threshold fairly high from the current Rs 20,00,000 can be made. However, the government argues that keeping a lower threshold allows the generation of greater revenue. Ultimately, the aptness of this threshold should be judged on the basis of not only revenue inflows to the government, but also the performance of small-scale industries in the future.

Table 8.2: Band-wise Turnover Distribution

Turnover Band (Rs)	*Total Turnover (in Rs Crore)*	*% of Total Turnover*
0–10 lakh	84,964	0.4
10 lakh–25 lakh	1,11,751	0.5
25 lakh–40 lakh	1,03,662	0.46
40 lakh–1 crore	4,46,671	1.98
1 crore–2 crore	7,12,837	3.16
2 crore–5 crore	13,41,213	5.95
5 crore–10 crore	13,07,752	5.8
10 crore–100 crore	46,92,026	20.82
Above 100 crore	1,37,26,108	60.93
Total	2,25,26,984	100

Source: Ministry of Finance (2015); Banerjee and Prasad (2017).

It also pertinent to note here that the threshold limits for major erstwhile indirect taxes—service tax, VAT and excise—were Rs 10 lakh, Rs 20 lakh and Rs 1.5 crore, respectively. There was also compulsory registration for interstate goods movement under the CST, regardless of turnover. This means that the problem of low registration thresholds is not new. But the number of people registered under GST far exceeds that from the previous tax regimes. Of the 1.03 crore taxpayers registered under GST till

March 2018, close to 40 per cent were newly registered entities not migrated from previous tax systems.[10] It is important to note that the government's assessment of increased revenue emanates not only from an increase in taxpayers, but also from effective checks on tax evasion. In that light, higher registration is a boon, which would allow speedy formalisation of the economy. Furthermore, an indirect benefit of such a registrant base expansion is the overflow of information regarding the business dealings of the registrants. Consequently, the government expects an increase in its direct tax revenues. Indeed, gross personal and corporate income tax collections have increased by 44 per cent and 17 per cent, respectively,[11] though not all of it can be attributed to GST. Table 8.3 provides the trends in gross personal and corporate income tax collections as a percentage of total direct tax collection and total tax collection (both direct and indirect tax).

Table 8.3: Corporate and Personal Tax as a Proportion of Direct and Total Taxes

	As a Percentage of Direct Tax		*As a Percentage of Total Tax*	
	Corporate Tax	*Personal Tax*	*Corporate Tax*	*Personal Tax*
1950–51	17%	58%	6%	21%
1960–61	27%	42%	8%	12%
1970–71	37%	47%	8%	10%
1980–81	40%	46%	7%	8%
1990–91	44%	44%	6%	6%
2000–01	50%	44%	12%	10%
2010–11	66%	31%	23%	11%
2013–14	61%	37%	21%	13%
2014–15	61%	37%	21%	13%
2015–16 (RE)	59%	38%	19%	12%
2016–17 (BE)	57%	40%	18%	13%

Source: Indian Public Finance Statistics (various editions).

Nevertheless, it is true that higher compliance costs can take a toll on small businesses. There have been a few studies that note how increased compliance costs have been hampering business activities. Banerjee and Prasad (2017: 19) note, 'While this goal [capturing maximum low-value transactions to formalise informal sector] is appreciable, compliance cost and cost of doing business should be commensurate to the profits earned.' Still, it is relevant to note that since GST has been on the horizon only for a year now, evidence related to its success or negative impact has been slim.

Input Credit Refunds

A GST regime is only as strong as its refunds system. Refunds are taxpayers' claim on state funds for the taxes paid by them on inputs, and when a claim is due, it should be paid by the government. The issue that the government generally grapples with regarding refunds is the curbing of fake refund claims. Germany, with a highly sophisticated tax administration, had struggled with a severe problem of fraud on account of illegitimate invoices for tax input credit purposes. So much so, that it was proposed that no refund would be processed unless the government receives satisfactory proof on the input tax credit claimed (Sinn et al. 2004).

Taxpayers often complain of late refunds, which create a working capital shortage. Reports of slow refunds on the part of the government to avoid bogus claims have been plentiful in Malaysia. Exporters have also raised similar complaints of severe shortage of working capital on account of delayed returns. Under the GST Regulations 2014, in Malaysia, tax input credit should be made within 14 and 18 working days for online and manual claim submission, respectively (Wong and Partners 2016). But the authorities have insisted that a full audit must be undertaken on companies' accounts before claims are settled,[12] which has, understandably, drawn sharp reactions from the business community. GST in Malaysia has generally not been a popular measure among the masses, with complaints ranging from increasing costs of living to sluggish growth of the economy.[13]

However, it should be acknowledged that some bad fish would remain in the tax system. Instead of complicating the whole system to curb them, a fine balance has to be established, maximising revenue and efficiency on the one hand, and minimising evasion (instead of aiming to eliminate it altogether) on the other. Curiously, delay in refund processing may not always be due to an overly cautious government wary of fraud and evasion. Sometimes, mismanagement on the part of the government can also cause it. In Jamaica, for example, the government has regularly delayed the payment of refunds, evidently due to lack of cash (Edmiston and Bird 2004).[14] In fact, many cash-strapped developing countries regularly run into the problem of erratic finances, spending when they have it (Caiden and Wildavsky 1980).

In India's case, studies regarding the efficiency or troubles with respect to the refund process are scant, and most evidence available is anecdotal. Claims exist in support of both the good and bad sides of the process. Just like Malaysia, Indian exporters have raised concerns about capital crunch due to refund delay. The refund dues of exporters have run into thousands of crores. A study by Tomar et al. (2018) also supports the hypothesis of the detrimental impact of GST on exports. They note,

> Prior to GST, the exporters were upfront exempted from paying any duties. Now, under GST, they are required to first pay the tax and later claim refunds... [Furthermore] the refunds filed in the month of July were sanctioned to the creditors only in late October and November... jeopardising the working capital requirements between filing and refunds. (ibid.: 2)

A Reserve Bank of India (RBI) analysis confirmed that industries engaged in exports did face a shortage in working capital on account of delayed refunds. This led to an increase in their short-term borrowings as they used up their cash and bank balances to cope with the capital crunch (RBI 2018a). This crunch was particularly severe for firms with high working capital to sales ratio. After the representatives of exporters escalated their plight with the relevant authorities,[15] the government announced various sops to alleviate exporters' concerns. The authorities also slowly paid back. Along with fast-tracking the refunds process, these measures were partly successful in achieving a rebound in export growth. The month of November 2017 saw a 30.55 per cent year-on-year growth in exports. There has still been sluggishness in some sectors, for example, apparel exports were down by roughly 14 per cent in January 2018.[16] But overall, there is evidence of improvement in exports health—goods export growth in India achieved a six-year high of 9.8 per cent in the year 2017–18.[17] In this context, it is relevant to note that not all refund delays can be attributed to the government. A large part of it occurs due to erroneous filings of returns by taxpayers through the GST portal.[18] Therefore, it is imperative to note that GST in India is still at a nascent stage. Time should be given to taxpayers to fully acclimatise themselves with the system before judging the efficacy of the refund process in GST.

Sub-national VAT

Given the high degree of fiscal autonomy that provincial governments enjoy in a federal system, federal governments the world over have developed numerous systems to divide fiscal powers relating to VAT. Upon careful study of VAT systems in numerous countries, Bird and Gendron (2001) identify different VAT arrangements between federal and provincial governments.

The two levels of government can decide to impose VAT on taxpayers completely independent of each other. The closest resemblance to this kind of system is found in Brazil. Brazil imposed a VAT for the federal government, and one each for the respective provincial governments. However, Brazil is a case study of how not to build a tax regime. It has a federal VAT (IPI) levied from 0 per cent to 365 per cent (depending on the classification of the goods), with multiple exemptions. Each state also has its own VAT (ICMS) with a wider tax base and its own rates (although the federal government may set the minimum rate).

There still exists a municipal service tax (ISS), a kind of sales tax, levied on services not taxed under ICMS. In addition, gross receipts contributions (PIS-PASEP and COFINS) are collected as social contributions on turnover basis (EY 2018). So many taxes with large band rates make the VAT system cryptic. Application of VAT on interstate transactions has also been a point of technical vagueness. Although there have been attempts in the past to rationalise the system and make it more coherent (Silvani and dos Santos 1996), much still remains to be done. As Bird and Gendron (2001: 24) noted after some reform efforts, 'eventually, however, the resulting patchwork quilt—perhaps a better analogy would be a blimp with a lot of chewing gum patches—became so unsatisfactory that sales tax reform has again risen high on the fiscal agenda in Brazil in recent years.'

Another arrangement could be of continued independence of federal and provincial VATs (as the aforementioned case), with different (or same) rates, but similar bases and a far greater degree of cooperation between them. An example of such a system is the Canadian GST-QST (Québec sales tax) case. GST is a VAT levied by the federal government, and QST is a VAT imposed by the province of Québec. The governments set the tax rates as well as the tax bases independently of each other, although the tax bases are almost similar. Some areas of aberration remained, which have been resolved over time. One such aberration was the cascading effect of QST. QST was charged on price plus GST, thereby taxing the tax. However, after multiple rounds of deliberations, effective from 1 January 2013, QST is no longer calculated on price plus GST (EY 2018). This understanding between the federal government of Canada and the provincial government of Québec is a fine example of a working dual VAT system since it avoided suffering from the usual problems associated with sub-national VATs, like lack of trust and coordination between the governments, jurisdictional issues and confusion in administration due to taxation at two levels.

One more form of understanding between two government levels is like the one found in Germany and Australia. In Germany, a single VAT is collected by the federal government, which is then distributed among the state governments based on a formula (Bird and Gendron 2001). In a way, the federal government collects the tax for the state governments. A similar process is followed in Australia as well. The VAT (called GST) is a federally levied tax in Australia. The Commonwealth Grants Commission devolves GST revenue among the states using its formula for fiscal capacity and basic expenditure equalisation. This revenue is then available for states, to be spent according to their own budgetary priorities (Bagchi 2007). This centralised VAT collection system has proven to be stable over the years, and it can provide important lessons for developing and transitional economies. However, this system vests a lot of authority with the federal government and might not be a natural choice in countries with strong provincial governments.

The Indian arrangement between the federal and state governments is most closely related to the Canadian GST-QST model. This resemblance occurs primarily because both the federal and the state governments in Canada have their own GSTs with similar tax bases. The same is true for India as well. GST in India is, in fact, divided into three types of rates—the central goods and services tax (CGST), the state goods and services tax (SGST) and the integrated goods and services tax (IGST). As the names suggest, the CGST is governed by the Central government and the SGST by the respective state governments or Union Territories. The IGST is governed by the Central government. The Central government divides the revenue collected through IGST between itself and various state governments.

There are, however, some important differences as well. In Canada, the Québec and federal governments have autonomy in deciding their own tax bases and rates. In India, the governments have sacrificed their fiscal independence in order to create one market. Changes in GST tax rates or base cannot take place without the approval of the GST Council, where both the Union and the states are represented.[19]

The two systems differ on the issue of tax administration as well. In the GST-QST framework, the regional Québec government administers both the taxes. In India, as noted earlier, different governments administer their respective tax systems. In fact, to avoid confusion, the taxpayer base itself has been clearly defined. Ninety per cent assesses below the annual turnover limit of 1.5 crore are under state jurisdiction, while the remaining 10 per cent fall under Union jurisdiction. For assesses above this limit, the division is equal.[20]

However, there are certain crucial implications that emanate from the Indian GST design. The most important one is the loss of fiscal independence of the states and the Union. Neither can decide on matters related to GST without the approval of the GST Council. Indirect taxes had been the backbone of state finances. The most important of these taxes were the state VATs, forming roughly two-thirds of state finances. This means that with the rollout of GST, states have agreed to lose control over three quarters of their finances and jointly manage it with other states and the Union government through the GST Council. The full impact of GST on state finances remains to be seen, and it will most certainly depend on its revenue buoyancy (Chakraborty et al. 2017). GST would also limit the effectiveness of taxation as a fiscal tool in the hands of states. Chakraborty (2017), however, argues that tax policy has long lost its effectiveness, given the globalised nature of our economies that force a convergence of tax rates. Nevertheless, the full import of such a grand fiscal reform on fiscal federalism will only be visible in the years to come.

Impact of GST on the Economy

Inflation

Before assessing the impact of a VAT/GST on inflation, it is pertinent to clarify what inflation means. Inflation is the rate of increase in the observed general price index between two time periods, i.e., a change in inflation implies a change in the rate of change of the general price level. In this context, Tait (1988) classifies the impact of VAT on inflation into four categories:

(a) the shift case, where the Consumer Price Index (CPI) reaches a new level (high or low, depending on whether the tax is increased or cut), although the rate of change of CPI remains unchanged; (b) the acceleration case, where the rate of change of CPI (inflation) changes; (c) the case of shift plus acceleration; and (d) little or no effect. Thus, a VAT that causes an increase in the CPI level in a particular period but does not change the rate of change of CPI in general can at best be called inflationary in that particular period only. For example, Tait cites the case of Denmark, which introduced VAT in July 1967. Before the introduction, the CPI rose from a trend of 90, 91, 92 and 93 to 100 and then continued on the pre-VAT trend.

Inflation due to the introduction (or increase) of an indirect tax (say, VAT) can occur primarily because of three reasons. First, increase in prices when the producers pass on the tax burden to the consumers. It is important to emphasise that a VAT is like any other form of indirect taxation—all things remaining constant, tax on a commodity is bound to raise its prices. The quantum of such a price rise then depends on the extent to which the supplier passes the raise on to the consumers. Even so, such an increase can only be sustained if there is commensurate increase in the demand for that good relative to the output level (Ruebling 1973). Similar dynamics play out at the macro level for general prices as well.

Second, the tendency of the buyers to advance purchases in order to avoid an expected price rise post the tax imposition. Such a practice allows the buyers to avoid increased prices after the tax increase. However, this causes an abrupt increase in demand, leading to a mild increase in prices, as sellers partially hike rates to take advantage of the higher demand. Thus, prices increase even before the tax is actually imposed. This phenomenon is called 'inflation smoothing' since a part of the inflation is brought forward before the tax actually takes effect. Germany saw this phenomenon unfolding when it increased the VAT rate from 16 per cent to 19 per cent on 1 January 2007 (Denninger and Carare 2008). Since the tax increase had been announced in advance, inflation in

Germany started rising before January. In fact, tobacco producers and importers had raised retail prices up to 5 per cent by as early as 1 October 2017, a full three months before the scheduled increase in VAT. A study by Deutsche Bundesbank (2008) notes that 'Year-on-year inflation for goods and services subject to the higher rate of VAT (excluding energy) went up from 0.2% in the first half of 2006 to 0.5% in the second half and from 1.9% in the first half of 2007 to 2.1% in the second half of the year.' However, it must be noted that other factors like increasing oil and food prices internationally also contributed to increase in inflation.

Box 8.1: Anti-profiteering in GST

Under section 171 of the CGST Act, 2017, the Government of India has constituted the National Anti-profiteering Authority. This authority is tasked to 'examine whether input tax credits availed by any registered person or the reduction in the tax rate have actually resulted in a commensurate reduction in the price of the goods or services or both supplied by him' (CGST Act 2017).

Any consumer can approach the Authority with documentary evidence for a non-transmission of benefits accruing on account of (a) and (b) to the buyers. The authority is empowered to direct the businesses to repay the amount of unpassed benefits along with interest, to impose penalties on the supplier or to order cancellation of registration of the seller, among other actions.

When the government of India announced its intention to include the anti-profiteering clause in the CGST Act, it drew widespread criticism. The critics were of the view that such a clause is retrograde and gives the impression of inspector raj. However, such practices on the part of governments are not new, and have been used the world over to check an unreasonable rise in prices post-VAT implementation and to allay public fear regarding inflation. The following are some instances where governments interfered and prevented excessive price increases on the part of manufacturers and sellers:

1. Ireland: The Irish National Prices Commission and Advisory Council on the Transition of VAT monitored the movement in prices of a wide range of goods after VAT implementation in 1972. They carried publicity campaigns informing buyers that there will

(*Contd*)

(*Box 8.1 contd*)

not be any material increase in the effective tax rate and asking them to report any overcharging ascribed to VAT on the part of sellers.

2. The Netherlands: The Dutch introduced VAT in 1969, and to fight the inflationary situation, the government brought a price freeze on 14 March 1969, compelling certain industries to roll back their price increases that were considered excessive. Furthermore, no increases in profit margins were permitted for a certain time period.
3. United Kingdom: The British Parliament introduced the Counter-Inflation Bill in 1973 before the adoption of VAT from 1 April 1973 to prevent undue increase in prices. This bill was drafted in consultation with the industry, with deliberations with the Confederation of British Industry and the Retail Consortium, and was not a unilateral move on the part of the government. According to the bill, a temporary price control could be enforced on receipt of a complaint for a particular good if it was found that the price rise did not correctly reflect the tax changes. The shopkeeper would be required to correct the price thereafter.
4. Australia: The Australian government empowered the Australian Competition and Consumer Commission (ACCC) to monitor price movements across a wide range of products, and also to take action against manufacturers and sellers who increase their prices that are inconsistent with the tax changes. The basic aim of this policy was to ensure that the people get full benefits from tax cuts, that they do not experience unduly high price rises and that they are not exploited or misguided by enterprises.

Source: Tait (1988); Nair and Eapen (2017); CGST Act (2017), available at http://gstcouncil.gov.in/sites/default/files/CGST.pdf (accessed 30 November 2019); https://www.livemint.com/Money/WnexrVFYD13jGdEZ46VS4N/Anti-profiteering-under-GST-A-leap-of-faith-for-consumers-a.html (accessed 30 November 2019).

Third, increase in prices due to a wage–price spiral. Workers want their wages to keep pace with rising inflation, and so they demand wage hikes. Sometimes, this increase forces suppliers to increase prices further, thus necessitating another round of wage hike demand to keep their real wages constant (Ruebling 1973).

This process is dangerous and can quickly spin out of control if not regulated properly, especially at places where unions are strong. It is curious to note here that a wage hike can happen before a tax imposition in response to a possible price rise, thus again causing inflation even before the tax has actually been levied. This has previously been observed in Denmark before the 1967 VAT introduction (Tait 1988).

In general, countries like Australia, New Zealand and Malaysia have experienced a spike in inflation post the VAT implementation. Australia's case can, however, fall into the no-effect category since a number of studies have concluded that the spike in inflation post-GST implementation was short and only limited to the September quarter of 2000 (Valadkhani and Layton 2004). Thereafter, the inflation returned to its pre-GST level. The Australian inflation spike was quick to show, yet very transitory in nature. GST was implemented on 1 July 2000 and its inflationary impacts were visible but limited to the September quarter only.

Nevertheless, the effect of inflation due to a tax can be managed. Even though a tax may increase the prices of some goods, the authorities can either reduce taxes on some other goods or provide separate set-offs or transfers to ease the burden of the taxes. This will leave the relative prices of the goods not too altered. Furthermore, in case there is an overall reduction in the tax burden, governments can also put in anti-profiteering provisos to ensure that the benefits are passed on to the final consumers. Box 8.1 discusses some instances from various countries where governments have intervened and prevented anti-profiteering activities on the part of manufacturers and sellers. It also discusses the anti-profiteering set-up put in place by the Union government in India.

Prior to the introduction of GST, the opinion regarding its inflationary nature in India was mixed. Some expected it to be deflationary or marginally inflationary at best. On the other hand, many commentators believed that prices would see an increase. However, to clearly understand GST's impact on CPI inflation, it is important to analyse the composition of the CPI basket.

Table 8.4 shows the weight distribution of different heads in the CPI basket for goods and services separately.

Table 8.4: Weights of Different Heads in the CPI Basket

Groups	*Total (%)*	*Services (%)*	*Goods (%)*
Food and Beverages	45.86	0.3242	45.5358
Pan, Tobacco and Intoxicants	2.38	0	2.38
Fuel and Light	6.84	0.51359	6.32641
Housing	10.07	10.06975	0.00025
Clothing and Footwear	6.53	0	6.53
Miscellaneous	28.32	12.45905	15.86095
Total	100	23.36659	76.63341

Source: Consumer Price Index—Changes in the Revised Series (Ministry of Statistics and Programme Implementation 2015); author's calculations.

It is clear from Table 8.4 that almost 23 per cent of the CPI basket is composed of services, with the remaining 77 per cent being goods. The food and beverages group mainly contains items like cereals, milk and milk products, fruits, vegetables and pulses. The goods part of this grouping has almost 46 per cent weightage in the CPI basket (the weight of services being negligent), falling either under the 0 per cent category or the 5 per cent one. Items under the 'fuel and light' head have been kept outside the purview of GST, and they continue to attract the same taxes as before. This means that they are unlikely to cause any incremental effect on inflation. Clothing and footwear fall under the 5 per cent or 12 per cent slab, depending on their prices. The goods portion of the 'miscellaneous' head contributes almost 16 per cent weight to the CPI basket and attracts tax rates in the slabs of 5 per cent, 12 per cent and 18 per cent. Only the 'pan, tobacco and intoxicants' section, which has a meagre 2.38 per cent weightage, lies under the 28 per cent category (these goods were taxed heavily under the earlier tax regime as well). But even of this 2.38 per cent weight, products like liquor and wine, which constitute almost 0.90 per cent in the CPI basket, are exempt. The services component forms almost 23 per cent of the overall CPI basket. However, more than half of it is exempted under various exemptions granted to health, education and housing services.

The aforementioned discussion reveals that roughly 30 per cent (parts of pan, tobacco and intoxicants; clothing and footwear; and miscellaneous goods and services) of the CPI basket is affected by GST, out of which it is only the services sector that has seen a substantial increase to 18 per cent under GST from the earlier 15 per cent service tax. On this count, therefore, inflationary pressures are expected to be substantially subdued, if at all present. In addition, availability of input tax credit further dampens possible prospects of any price rise. However, it must be noted that while there might be goods that are either kept out of the GST purview or have seen a reduction in tax rates, producers of those goods might still see rising costs due to higher taxes on the inputs used. For example, the beer industry used to pay excise duty, sales tax and VAT at the rate of 12–15 per cent. But under GST, most inputs fall under the 18 per cent bracket.[21] Such examples can be seen in other industries as well. An industry-wise analysis can present a much better picture of GST's impact on inflation, as it will investigate not only the price effect of taxes on industry-specific inputs, but also the number of stages of production required for manufacturing that good.

It is important to scrutinise other considerations weighing on inflation, lest their impact be wrongly attributed to GST. The macroeconomic scenario in a country is one such determinant that significantly alters the behaviour of inflation. In India's case, the implementation of GST happened during a period of continuous increase in the international prices of crude oil, which is historically a major contributor to inflation due to its use as fuel and its cascading impact on the prices of other commodities. Figure 8.1 tracks the movement of crude oil prices and year-on-year CPI inflation before and after the introduction of GST.

Figure 8.1: Y-O-Y CPI and Crude Oil Prices

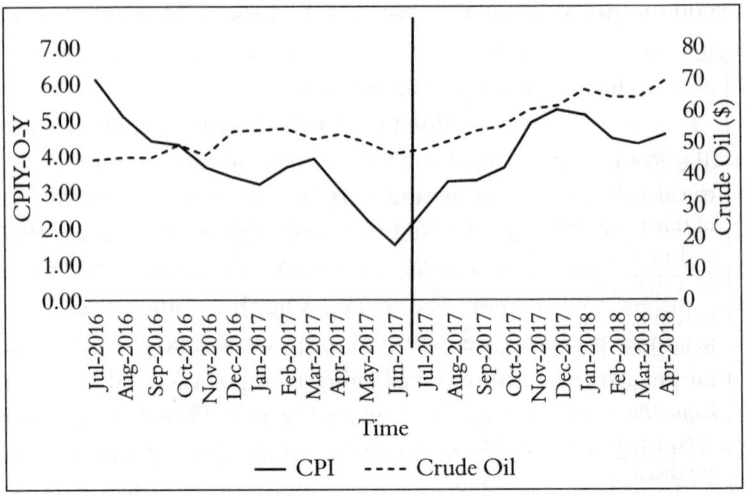

Source: Ministry of Statistics and Programme Implementation, http://164.100.34.62:8080/TimeSeries_2012.aspx (accessed 22 July 2018); https://in.investing.com/currencies/wti-usd-historical-data (accessed 22 July 2018).

Figure 8.1 indicates a positive correlation between crude oil prices and inflation. Notice that inflation had started rising not after the introduction of GST in July 2017 but in June 2017, roughly the same time as crude oil prices also started rising. This is not to say that GST has not been inflationary. Some evidence suggests that it has contributed to the inching up of inflation as well, but its effect is very limited. The market note released by the State Bank of India (SBI) research in September 2017 ascribed just 12 basis points to GST out of the 190 basis points jump in headline CPI inflation, i.e., only 6.3 per cent of the rise in inflation was attributable to GST in the initial few months.[22] Further, in Figure 8.1, a sharp rise and then a moderation in CPI around the months October to February are mainly attributable to the seasonal features of prices of food items in the CPI basket, most of which lie in the 0 per cent or 5 per cent GST slab. The implementation of the Seventh Pay Commission has also led to increased prices of components of the CPI basket due to a strong demand in the economy (RBI 2017a, 2018b).[23]

Box 8.2: Impact of GST on the Indian Economy—
An RBI Perspective

The Reserve Bank of India (RBI) in its *Annual Report 2017–18* has elucidated on the myriad effects of GST on the Indian economy. Reforms of this magnitude happen rarely in a country, and thus its effects (positive and negative) were felt and observed everywhere. The implementation of GST was marked by some initial complications, confusions and bottlenecks, which caused an economic slowdown in many sectors and industries. Based on their nature, the impacts of GST on the economy can be segregated into two kinds—short term and long term. As is clear from the *Annual Report*, the short-term impacts of GST have mostly been negative effects emanating from the initial teething issues, which are discussed next:

1. Uncertainties relating to GST implementation caused a transient slowdown in the first quarter of 2017–18. However, fixed investment (indicative of the scale of economic activity) rebounded the very next quarter and 'sustained momentum for the rest of the year' (p. 12). GST shocks were also cushioned by the strong performance of the private final consumption expenditure, which rode high on the fillip provided by the enhanced pays under the Seventh Central Pay Commission Rewards (p. 15).
2. There was deceleration in the sales growth in various manufacturing firms in the first quarter of 2017–18, possibly due to destocking ahead of GST implementation. However, following the economy-wide trend, sales growth rebounded from the second quarter (p. 22).
3. Government finances also faced the pinch from the lingering effects of demonetisation and the initial bottlenecks from GST. They were marked by deviation from deficit targets. Among other reasons, the RBI *Annual Report* (p. 65) cited late implementation of GST and the initial implementation problems associated with it as crucial pressure points. Although eventually the indirect tax collections exceeded previous years' collections, the buoyancy was compromised, resulting in a dip in the tax-to-GDP ratio. However, revenue receipts at the state level are expected to increase in future

(*Contd*)

(*Box 8.2 contd*)

on account of central transfers and states' own tax revenue (p. 68). Further, any shortfalls could be met via increased revenue from a broadened GST base and the anti-evasion e-way bill as well (p. 71). Expounding on the fiscal position of the state budgets, the report expresses confidence that the GST compensation revenue from the Union will cushion the tight fiscal position of the states that arose partly on account of populist measures like the farm loan waivers in some states (p. 7).

4. Even the external sector did not go unaffected by GST. As noted in the RBI *Annual Report*, the Indian economy could not take full advantage of the rising global demand due to its internal supply-side bottlenecks following demonetisation and GST implementation. In particular, GST caused a major working capital issue for exporters. In the initial few months post-GST, the refunds for the input tax credit were slow to come by, and exporters had to resort to short-term borrowing to wade through this liquidity squeeze (p. 73). While RBI, in its earlier publication (*Monetary Policy Report*, RBI 2017b), had already stated that it does not expect a significant impact of GST on inflation, it does note that rate reduction on various commodities by the GST Council helped in softening inflation following a seven-month high in October.
5. The government also had to borrow additionally (in the form of cash management bills) to provide against the uncertainty regarding the GST revenue stream (p. 142).

Thus, as stated earlier, the impact of a totally new tax system and the ensuing uncertainties led to a squeeze in many parts of the economy. The *Annual Report* argues that once GST settles, the benefits will become more visible. The report exudes confidence that 'the GST may gradually expand revenues as it stabilises and gains traction' (p. 6). The equity markets have largely been highly optimistic about GST. They began the year on a positive note due to the finalisation of the GST rates, among other things (p. 59). Indices more directly concerned with the longer-term impact of GST also responded positively. For example, the softening bias seen in the gilt yields reduced after the passage of the GST Bill (p. 55). Thus, the central bank has taken a strong positive stand on the future impressions of GST on the economy.

Source: RBI (2018a).

Economic Growth

Economy-wide effects of a VAT are difficult to gauge, and nothing as such can be said with certainty. There are definite efficiency and administrative gains when a cascading indirect tax regime is replaced with VAT. But its effects on economic growth are far from clear. If a VAT increases government revenue, then theoretically, it is possible that private consumption is reduced since the public would be paying more in taxes than before. But the government might use such extra revenue to reduce its fiscal deficit or finance any scheme. The growth effect then depends upon the individual multipliers of spending through either private consumption or government consumption. Moreover, a lot also depends on how the private sector behaves in response to such increase in government spending. The expansion might crowd out private investment and could actually depress private investment in the economy, or a reduction in fiscal deficit might reduce interest rates and, thus, boost private investment. Similarly, price rise in some items might prompt households to reduce their consumption (a lot depends on the price elasticity of demand of the good). On the contrary, tax rate reduction or increase in price may induce the private sector to supply more, leading to better gross output (Ruebling 1973). The private sector might also benefit from the lower logistics costs and hindrance-free movement of goods. Thus, the effect of VAT on the economy rests on many distinct factors and nothing in particular can be said with certainty. We next look at VAT's effect on investment, ease of doing business and international trade as an effort to understand VAT's impact on growth.

Investment and Ease of Doing Business

There are various theoretical general equilibrium models that establish channels through which taxation can affect economic growth. However, the empirical relation between the two has been, at best, weak (Myles 2000). But what makes taxes critical is their impact on the decision-making of economic agents. Taxes affect household decisions to save and firms' decisions regarding investment, production and trade.[24] Moreover, the effect of tax levels and structures becomes visible on the overall economic well-being of the agents (OECD 2010).

A variable that has a direct bearing on growth and is affected by tax is investment. An indirect tax can be an important factor in deciding the extent of investment in a sector or the economy in general. A usual sales tax taxes the inputs involved in the production process as well, including capital inputs. A tax on capital perversely affects the investment decisions of firms and can even lead to slowing down or reduction in investment. A VAT, on the other hand, through its input credit mechanism, does not tax inputs of any kind, including capital inputs. This leads to a favourable treatment towards capital goods in a VAT regime as compared to a non-VAT regime, which becomes a very important factor in a firm's investment decision. But does a VAT really lead to better investment than a non-VAT regime where tax cascades? Bird and Smart (2008) check this hypothesis for Canada, where five states had a retail sales tax (RST) and four states had a VAT. The non-VAT states worked as a counterfactual, showing the normal course without a VAT intervention. Bird and Smart (ibid.) observe that post-1997 (the reform year), the reforming states saw a rise in their per capita investment relative to the non-reforming states. They also note that this rise slowed or reversed after 1999, which is expected, since a reduction in the effective tax on capital goods should lead to a permanent rise in the capital stock and not a continuous increase.

The major point to note here is the favourable treatment that inputs receive in a VAT regime. A more narrow analysis with regard to input treatment was done by Wittwer and Anderson (2001) for the Australian wine industry. They project an expansion in the industry, which is mainly attributable to input cost reductions.

Another channel for the growth impact of a VAT is through efficiency. VAT makes businesses efficient through non-cascading of taxes and simplicity in the system. Simplicity is per se a non-economic variable. It relates more to the administrative side of taxation and only implicitly affects the working of a business. However, it is extremely crucial since a simple and workable tax system, without the customary rigmarole associated, reduces an entrepreneur's time on tax planning and makes that time available for more important business-related activities.

Another important feature of VAT is the ensuing uniformity of indirect tax laws across the reforming state. This may not be true for every country, since in Canada, as noted earlier, different states have somewhat differing tax systems. However, it applies well to states that have harmonised their tax jurisdictions, like Australia, New Zealand and India. Leemput (2016) estimates that internal trade barriers in India constitute 40 per cent of the total trade cost on average. Due to this, logistics costs of Indian industries are expected to reduce by 10–12 per cent.[25] This is expected to increase the productivity of businesses, including international traders. Leemput and Wiencek (2017) estimate that an average GST rate of 20 per cent would increase GDP by 3.1 per cent, whereas a GST rate of 16 per cent is estimated to increase GDP by 4.2 per cent, thereby expecting a significant positive impact of GST on the Indian economy. This is also in agreement with the National Council of Applied Economic Research (NCAER 2009)[26] prediction of expansion in GDP post-GST. The impact of GST on the Indian economy, along with its effects on other sectors of the economy, were discussed by the RBI (2018a) in its *Annual Report 2017–18*, presented in Box 8.2.

It seems reasonable to think that a VAT would lead to better economic growth. However, as noted earlier, the answer is not so simple and still requires some qualifications. Revenue neutrality and broad basing are important aspects for the success of VAT. Generally, moving from a production-based tax system to a consumption-based VAT requires that the tax rate on some commodities be increased and that on others be decreased. This is done to make the tax revenue neutral. Due to this, some industries might experience contraction due to increased taxation,[27] while others might see an expansion. However, the overall impact will depend on the magnitude of each of the opposite effects.

International Trade

The one sphere where VAT's impact is fairly clear and yet highly misunderstood is international trade. Various pundits and politicians, including former US President Bill Clinton, have claimed over the years that a VAT promotes exports and discourages imports, thus pitting a country favourably against its international competitors. This, they say, happens because exports are zero rated and exporters get a refund on the tax paid, whereas imports are taxed at the same rate as domestically manufactured goods, giving them a level playing field.[28] However, nothing can be farther from the truth. It is well-accepted among economists that theoretically, VAT does not favour or discriminate against exports or imports. Feldstein and Krugman (1989: 2) show that barring the very short run, a VAT has no effect on exports or imports as 'the exchange rates or domestic prices adjust to offset the effect of tax on relative prices of domestic and foreign goods'. Upon the introduction of VAT, countries like Italy, Sweden or the UK did not see any significant increase in exports. Even in countries like Germany, which did see a rise in exports, it was attributable significantly to the lower domestic demand and higher labour productivity. Generally, world demand and exchange rate fluctuations play a far more significant role in international trade in comparison to paltry gains, if any, available from a shift to VAT. In fact, Desai and Hines (2005) find evidence that countries with a VAT regime have 33 per cent less exports than those that do not have it. This negative correlation is stronger in the case of low-income countries. They further find that greater VAT revenue is associated with fewer exports. This may be due to the administrative bottlenecks present, which are generally not faced by richer countries. Keen and Syed (2006), in their analysis of Organisation for Economic Co-operation and Development (OECD) countries, conclude that VAT is generally trade-neutral. Ups and down in the trade may be more affected by consumption patterns and corporate tax rather than VAT.

Thus, the evidence of VAT's impact on international trade shows that it will either have no effect, or will have a negative effect.

However, it is to be noted here that results obtained from aggregate data across many countries present an average picture. The individual experience of the countries may differ from the average on account of various country-specific factors, which may not reflect anything on VAT in general.

Government Revenue

The design of a VAT (or GST) is such that it induces taxpayers to pay their taxes. In order to take advantage of the input tax credit, the buyer furnishes documents to prove purchases, which are then matched against the documents proving sales of the supplier. This self-enforcing mechanism ensures limited leakages in the system. Since VAT is generally introduced as a revenue-neutral tax, most governments hope to curb evasion of this tax and earn more revenue than the previous tax system. Based on the nature of the supply chain under VAT, transactions can be divided into two parts: (a) intermediary transactions between firms, and (b) final transactions between firms and consumers. The former is generally covered by a paper trail (physical or electronic) since it is crucial to claim the input credit, but the latter type experiences fewer paper trails as the final consumers do not have the same incentive to request receipts. These transactions, therefore, are generally the weakest link in the chain. In this respect, a study done by Pomeranz (2015) for Chile presents evidence that VAT increases compliance among firms for transactions that are covered by a paper trail. Chilean tax authorities sent letters that indicated an increased audit probability to 1,00,000 randomly selected firms as part of the study. This caused firms' tax payments for sales to final consumers to increase but did not have much effect on the sales that were already covered under the paper trails, i.e., intermediary sales. This shows that VAT is effective in increasing compliance and, therefore, government revenue. There are similar country-specific examples that support the hypothesis that a VAT is effective in increasing government revenue.

Evidence shows that the presence of VAT is associated with higher government revenue in many countries. There are deviators as well, but they appear more the exception than the rule. Ebrill et al. (2001) calculated the revenue difference between VAT and prior sales tax regimes in different regions as a percentage of GDP (Table 8.5). The extra revenue earned by various countries is striking, with most gains in the Americas and various small island countries. A significant outlier in 'Central and Eastern Europe and Central Asia' is also present, but it has more to do with the economic transition that these countries were undergoing, resulting in a general decline in the tax to GDP ratio trend.

Table 8.5: Revenue Differences between VAT and Previous Tax Regimes as a Percentage of GDP

Sub-Saharan Africa	*Asia and Pacific*	*Central and Eastern Europe and Central Asia*	*Americas*	*EU*	*North Africa and Middle East*	*Small Islands*	*Average*
1.10	0.70	–1.88	1.42	1.05	0.10	1.96	1.1

Source: Ebrill et al. (2001).

Much earlier, Nellor (1987) had analysed VAT's impact on the tax to GDP ratio for 11 European countries. He found that the sample countries had experienced statistically significant increases in the tax to GDP ratio post-VAT implementation. However, qualifications are in order for such results, as Nellor himself notes. Each country is affected by its individual characteristics, which are supressed in the aggregate analysis. Moreover, results point to an increase in the tax revenue post-VAT, but do not specifically point out any inherent revenue-earning characteristics of VAT itself. Various related factors like the tax's design, the efficiency in tax administration, the level of development in the country, and other country-specific factors are extremely crucial to the tax performance. For example, Bogetic and Hassan (1993) found that countries with a simpler VAT regime tend to earn a greater revenue than those with a relatively complex one. Specifically, they argue that 'for value-added tax to provide superior revenues, it should be levied in a single rate on as broad a base as possible' (ibid.: 2).

The reason for such a finding might be that numerous rates increase the administrative costs of enforcing tax laws. They also increase compliance costs since multiple rates create confusion regarding the classification of different items under different rates.

A more concrete example of how VAT revenues are greatly affected by country-specific factors is Ukraine (Bird and Gendron 2007). VAT revenue as a proportion of GDP has declined steadily in Ukraine. From 1998 to 2004, its GDP rose by 49 per cent, but VAT revenue as a share of GDP fell by 33 per cent. There is no general consensus on the value of VAT revenue elasticity of GDP growth (percentage change in VAT revenue in response to a percentage change in GDP), but at 0.38, Ukraine's VAT revenue elasticity to GDP growth is abysmally low. Better efficiency in tax administration is a common policy advice that Ukraine receives in this regard.

A study in the International Tax Dialogue (2005) points out certain corollaries to the VAT and government revenue relation. A positive relation is found to be stronger at higher levels of per capita GDP and at a lower share of agriculture in GDP (as agriculture is generally the part of GDP that is exempt). Also, the revenue-generating capacity of VAT depends significantly on the importance of internal trade in the economy. The higher the importance of internal trade, the greater the gains from a smooth and unified market created after the removal of internal trade barriers.

However, a more important question to ask in this context is: Do governments in countries with VAT earn more revenue than those without it? The evidence on this front is mixed. Keen and Lockwood (2006) find a weak relationship between the presence of VAT and a higher tax to GDP ratio, with most robust and exhaustive models failing to confirm such a relationship beyond doubt. Keen and Lockwood (2007) again test a similar hypothesis, in which they note that the sign of revenue impact on VAT adoption is generally ambiguous.

However, to fully understand the performance of VAT, a qualitative analysis of the revenue is necessary. VAT revenue can be increased by (a) increasing the tax rate, (b) improving VAT design, (c) expanding the tax base, and/or (d) improving efficiency. Increasing the tax rate should be avoided when there remains scope for improvements in other categories, and it should be used as a last resort. C-efficiency is a ratio that allows us to measure the coverage and subsequently the performance of VAT in an economy. It is defined as the ratio of the actual VAT revenue to the revenue accruable if the standard VAT rate was applicable to all consumption:

$$E^C = \frac{V}{tC}$$

where E^C is the C-efficiency, V is the total VAT revenue, t is the standard VAT rate and C is the total consumption. This ratio thus tells the gap between actual revenue and the revenue possible if all consumption was taxed in the economy at the standard rate. The importance of this ratio and the need for governments to improve can be gauged by returning to our earlier example of Ukraine. It is estimated that if VAT actually taxed all final household consumption in Ukraine in 2004, it would have raised an additional 4.2 per cent of the GDP (Bird and Gendron 2007).

In a more recent and comprehensive analysis, Keen (2013) investigates the main drivers of changes in the VAT revenue in low-income, middle-income, upper-income and high-income countries for the period 1993–2010, and goes on to note that C-efficiency is by far the most important driver in VAT revenue and that changes in the standard rate have played second fiddle to C-efficiency. This means that countries have tried to improve their tax regime to generate more revenue by broadening their tax bases rather than indiscriminately resorting to increasing the tax rate. Keen (ibid.) further notes that C-efficiency in general has increased across countries in the 1993–2010 period. However, he notes that region-wise analysis of the C-efficiency suggests that in some regions, mostly the developing countries in Africa, Middle East and Central Asia, and the countries in Asia-Pacific, the scope of VAT has gradually been narrowed and consequently their

C-efficiency has fallen. On the contrary, in European countries, VAT tax bases have slowly expanded.

Thus, one thing is evident from the preceding discussion: it is not always clear if a VAT will increase the tax revenue of the government.[29] And to garner more revenue from a VAT once it is in place, broadening of the base is definitely a better strategy. Raising VAT rates to compensate for revenue shortfalls will only increase incentives to evade taxes in the long run.

Notes

1. https://www.orfonline.org/expert-speak/gst-a-marathon-not-a-100-metre-dash/ (accessed 16 August 2018).
2. https://www.ey.com/gl/en/services/tax/worldwide-vat--gst-and-sales-tax-guide---rates/ (accessed 16 August 2018).
3. GST in the country covers almost all goods and services. Only certain financial services, sale and lease of residential properties, and sale and import of qualifying investment metals are exempt from GST. Export of goods and international services are zero-rated (Shang and Leng 2014).
4. GST is to be raised from 7 per cent to 9 per cent sometime between 2021 and 2025 (https://www.straitstimes.com/singapore/singapore-budget-2018-gst-to-be-raised-from-7-to-9-sometime-between-2021-and-2025 [accessed 16 August 2018]).
5. Zero-rating can generally be distinguished from exemptions in the sense that it is consistent with the principle of non-cascadation, while exemptions are not.
6. https://taxguru.in/goods-and-service-tax/nil-rated-rated-nontaxable-exempt-supplies-gst.html (accessed 20 August 2018).
7. https://www.livemint.com/Politics/nSNsYyctSazqC5jLcMj4UN/GST-has-brought-growth-simplicity-PM-Narendra-Modi.html (accessed 20 August 2018).
8. https://timesofindia.indiatimes.com/business/india-business/gst-council-to-continue-rationalising-rates-shukla/articleshow/60985051.cms (accessed 20 August 2018).
9. http://www.gstcouncil.gov.in/sites/default/files/CEA-rpt-rnr.pdf (accessed 21 August 2018).

10. https://economictimes.indiatimes.com/news/economy/policy/over-1-03-crore-businesses-registered-under-gst-government/articleshow/63232433.cms (accessed 22 August 2018).
11. https://economictimes.indiatimes.com/news/economy/policy/arun-jaitley-hints-at-rationalising-gst-rates-as-revenues-surge/articleshow/64820692.cms (accessed 22 August 2018).
12. https://www.thestar.com.my/metro/smebiz/news/2015/07/06/late-gst-refunds-a-headache/ (accessed 29 August 2018).
13. The new Mahathir government announced the reduction of the GST rate from 6 per cent to 0 per cent, effectively abolishing it.
14. This despite the fact that an interest of 2.5 per cent per month has to be paid on refunds not paid within 90 days.
15. https://www.deccanchronicle.com/business/economy/280917/industry-exporters-take-up-timely-refund-of-duties-with-arun-jaitley.html (accessed 31 August 2018).
16. https://www.timesnownews.com/business-economy/economy/article/one-year-of-gst-indias-garment-industry-suffering-from-gst-refund-delays/248264 (accessed 31 August 2018).
17. https://www.financialexpress.com/economy/what-gst-refund-problem-indias-goods-export-growth-seen-at-6-year-high/1133095/ (accessed 31 August 2018).
18. https://www.businesstoday.in/current/policy/delay-in-gst-refunds-to-exporters-smaller-businesses-struggle-for-capital/story/272323.html (accessed 31 August 2018).
19. http://www.gstcouncil.gov.in/gst-council (accessed 4 September 2018).
20. https://economictimes.indiatimes.com/news/economy/policy/gst-centre-states-to-divide-taxpayer-base/articleshow/60786483.cms (accessed 4 September 2018).
21. https://economictimes.indiatimes.com/markets/stocks/news/alcohol-out-of-gst-for-now-but-beer-will-still-get-costlier/articleshow/58818443.cms (accessed 7 September 2018).
22. https://thewire.in/economy/explains-indias-five-month-inflation-high (accessed 7 September 2018).
23. For estimates of the impact of GST on CPI, see RBI (2017b).
24. The list is not exhaustive.
25. http://pib.nic.in/newsite/PrintRelease.aspx?relid=169021 (accessed 13 September 2018).
26. The report was prepared by NCAER for the Thirteenth Finance Commission of India.

27. Miki (2011) finds a negative relationship between VAT rate change and economic growth for a panel of 14 developed countries.
28. Even the Taskforce on Goods and Services Tax in its report (Thirteenth Finance Commission 2009) had argued on similar lines.
29. However, due to several factors, VAT is generally thought of as a 'money machine', i.e., it is seen as an effective tool to boost indirect tax revenue. In the United States, the general discourse on VAT revolves not around whether it will bring more money to the governments, but rather that it will unnecessarily bring more money. This situation, it is argued, might lead to a larger government (in terms of its expenditure) and encourage spending money in sectors that should otherwise be left to the private sector.

Conclusion

Goods and services tax (GST) has been a landmark tax reform in Indian taxation history. And naturally, a lot has been said about it already. It is almost one-and-a-half years old now. Since its introduction on 1 July 2017, the expectations around it have only increased. The most cited advantages of a GST-type tax are greater efficiency and simplification of the tax regime. At the same time, various transitional challenges have resulted in cynicism around the tax. Thus, it is crucial to analyse the various impacts, shortfalls and successes of this shift in tax policy. So in such a vein, this book has tried to document and analyse the efforts that went into making GST, systematically elucidate the apprehensions regarding its implementation and carefully assess its performance, particularly on the revenue front, based on the available data. It has also discussed India's indirect tax reform journey since independence, which has finally culminated in GST. It is kosher to say here that while a lot is said about the ideal structure, a perfect GST is a mirage—it is visible and yet it does not exist.

As has already been noted elsewhere in the book, indirect tax has traditionally been the most important source of tax revenue for governments. Economists prescribe that as a country develops, direct tax should unsettle indirect taxes as the leading revenue earner, i.e., less and less money should be derived from the inherently regressive indirect taxes. Yet, even in 2016–17, indirect taxes constituted 11.95 per cent of the gross domestic product (GDP), while direct taxes made up just 5.65 per cent of the GDP of India. For a long time after independence, indirect taxation was mainly considered just a tool for revenue and not a means to stimulate economic growth. Consequently, it did not undergo major reform processes and remained archaic for a very long time. After the 1970s, various committees were set up that recommended comprehensive reforms, many of which have been implemented. Subsequently, over the years, many changes have been made to indirect taxation, which ultimately culminated in a partial value-added tax (VAT) system for central excise and replaced the sales tax on goods at the state level in 2005. Service tax was introduced in India in 1994 by the Union government and the coverage of service tax increased over the years. In 2012, a negative list of services was introduced, implying a universal application of service tax in the country.

The current GST structure is a result of long and exhausting negotiations between the Union and the state governments. It has been considered the single-largest indirect tax reform since independence. If successfully implemented, its benefits are undeniable. It will propel India into a unified market, bring a uniform system of indirect taxation across the country and remove a plethora of state-specific levies. It is supposed to bring in efficiency in business operations, which will have a positive impact on economic growth.

GST also makes extensive use of technology. The entire GST network is reliant on it. The e-way bill is an important part of that ecosystem as it puts the movement of goods in sight of the tax administration, i.e., subsequent to the removal of checkposts at state borders, e-way bills provide a system of real-time tracking of goods consignments. Moreover, these bills get auto populated in the suppliers' GST returns (which earlier had to be manually checked). All this provides a huge fillip to the efforts against tax evasion (Chapter 6).[1] Moreover, since everything is online, and the format of an e-way bill is the same across the country, the time spent in checking transit documents and the confusion arising from different procedures in different states is eliminated.

Impacts

The government is really hopeful that its tax earnings would be significantly increased through GST. As noted earlier, the fulfilment of increased revenue is extremely crucial given the large-scale development expenditure required to fuel the economy. In this book, we have examined the relationship between GST and government revenue (Chapter 4). We have emphasised that simplicity of the tax regime is key to its better performance. Although we have carried out a preliminary analysis on the revenue front of GST for India, it still applies that every result (positive or negative) in the initial stages of GST should be read with utmost caution.

Other important areas of the impact of GST are inflation and economic growth (Chapter 8). GST has mostly proved to be non-inflationary. This has been supported by numerous studies in the Reserve Bank of India (RBI) and the private sector. As far as the impact of GST on economic growth is concerned, the relationship is foggy and unclear. The impact of GST depends largely on how it is implemented, i.e., the operational and executional aspects are just as important as the structural and design features. Further, the quantum of impact of GST on the economy depends on various country-specific factors as well as a wide array of other factors. Though various studies have been able to establish the link between GST and growth, this linkage is weak at best. In India, the short-term impact of GST has no doubt been negative. Teething problems, lack of awareness among taxpayers and frequent changing of rules are some of the main reasons for this.

One of the most important results expected from GST is the gradual reduction of fiscal disparities across states. Since most taxes earlier were production-based, a major chunk of the tax revenue was earned by producer states like Gujarat, Maharashtra and Tamil Nadu. However, since GST is a destination-based tax, taxes will now be collected by the states where the consumption takes place. This will help the poor consuming states like Uttar Pradesh, Bihar and Madhya Pradesh. However, to placate the apprehensions of the states regarding the consequent revenue loss, the Centre has agreed to compensate any shortfall in revenues for up to five years post the GST implementation.

However, the Indian GST is a model that reflects the complexities of a tax reform of such a magnitude and their subsequent resolution. Yet, some aspects of the tax design are in contradiction to the simplicity GST promises. In many cases, therefore, the results have been less than desired.

The rules regarding GST, tax rates and various exemptions are still changing, which makes it difficult to judge the performance of GST over the past one-and-a-half years comprehensively. It is important that the system be allowed to settle down and the people be given sufficient time to acclimatise themselves to the change. However, from the early data available on GST, some conclusions can still be drawn. GST has been quite successful in bringing previously unregistered businesses into the GST network. But on the other hand, taxpayers who filed returns are around 66 per cent of the total taxpayers on average. This means that while GST has been successful in bringing more businesses into the tax net, making them actually pay the taxes is still a work in progress.

Another important impact of GST is the increased pressure on the tax administration. This is because small businesses make up a significant proportion of the registrant base and yet the actual tax contribution from them is relatively miniscule. The world over, the situation is similar—a few large taxpayers pay most of the tax, while the rest are small and insignificant. Therefore, one argument has been to let go of these taxpayers, relieve the administration of high burden and focus on better serving the bigger taxpayers. This requires a careful setting of the registration threshold so that too many are not included. Another related feature is the increased compliance of small businesses. While a carefully set registration threshold takes care of it partially, research has shown that smaller firms face relatively larger compliance costs in relation to their operations. The composition scheme in India is a measure brought in to favour such small firms. However, initial data shows that a significant proportion of dealers below the threshold have not opted for the composition scheme and have registered under GST.

There is no doubt that GST has and will continue to have an impact on all sectors of the economy. The informal sector is of particular concern here, because it absorbs close to four-fifths of the total workforce in the country (Chapter 5). Impact of GST on the informal sector has been the increase in their GST registration on the portal. This means that more and more businesses are becoming part of the formal supply chain. Many commentators have linked this to increasing formalisation of the economy. However, things should be interpreted with caution here, as formalisation through GST registration does not mean a formalisation of jobs for a business set-up. It just means that the government can now collect taxes from such a business.

There are some nuanced issues that have arisen after GST has taken shape. One such is the blunting of tax policy as a fiscal tool for states (Chapter 3). It is true that the larger interests of the nation have taken precedence over individual state interests. But there is a danger of the independent and sometimes extraordinary financial needs of states being totally sidelined since tax policies of the Union and the states have fused and become the prerogative of a national decision-making body—the GST Council. GST also changes the tax relations between the Centre and states. Taxes have been the prerogative of both the Centre and the states. However, GST takes away that power and vests it with the GST Council, which is now responsible for the tax regimen of the Centre and all the states.

The treatment of the proceeds from the integrated goods and services tax (IGST) is also a major concern. Fifty per cent of the IGST collections are basically state revenues collected by the Centre for distribution. This collection is against interstate movement of goods and services and, thus, should be distributed according to the place/state of supply (the location of the delivery of goods or services). But, as has been noted elsewhere, it is disbursed on the devolution principle of the Fourteenth Finance Commission as the place of supply could not be determined for a large part of the IGST revenue. This implies that technology still needs refinement so that one is able to administer the place of supply rule easily.

THE WAY FORWARD

We have discussed various aspects of GST as well as some of the issues that have arisen from its implementation. The future holds a lot for GST, both in terms of opportunities and challenges. It is upon the administrators to clearly foresee the challenges and recognise the opportunities for better governance of the tax. Some such possibilities are discussed below.

In the Indian context, GST is relatively new and there is still a lot of scope for rationalisation. Incomplete coverage of goods and services and too many rates are issues at the top of the list. Although multiple rates and exemptions are part of the government's attempt to cater to the apprehensions of the states, in a larger context, they reduce the efficiency of GST. Thus, persistent base broadening is required, so that eventually the GST revenue ratio in India increases.

It is also important to gradually enhance the scope of GST to cover more and more sectors in the economy. This is crucial as it will eliminate the complexity and confusion arising from the differential treatment of covered and uncovered commodities. The coverage of petrol and petroleum products, which have been left out of GST's purview, is a case in point. Similarly, railways should also eventually be brought under GST to provide a level playing field to the various modes of transport.

A possible grey area relates to the anti-profiteering clause in the GST Act. While it is commendable that the intent of providing maximum benefits of a tax cut to the public has been given a legal basis, the guidelines regarding the application of such a provision remain unclear. The private sector has complained about the lack of clarity regarding the application of anti-profiteering rules. There is confusion about whether any definite method regarding the computation of benefit has to be passed, the time period within which this has to be done, and whether any specific records have to be maintained.

Another important point is the slow dilution of the mission of GST—simplification of the tax regime by eliminating multiple taxes and keeping only a few. The tendency to increase revenue through different measures is compromising the core principle of GST. In the recent past, Kerala has lobbied for a cess to garner extra revenue in the aftermath of the devastating floods. Similarly, in February, in place of the education cess and secondary and higher education cess, the government introduced the social welfare cess on imported goods. Recently, Madhya Pradesh allowed local bodies to levy an entertainment tax, thus negating the abolition of the entertainment tax at the state level. So there have been tendencies in small pockets to compromise the agenda of GST when faced with a tight fiscal position. This requires resolution. Limited fiscal autonomy with a floor rate of state goods and services tax (SGST) could bring that flexibility in the tax system and can prevent proliferation of new taxes.

One of the foremost expectations from GST was the realisation of 'one nation' in its truest sense, i.e., unhindered movement of goods and services in the country. While GST has mostly ensured this for the commercial side of things, some more nuanced gaps relating to the regulation and taxation of vehicles (and not goods) still exist, waiting to be plugged. With respect to the movement of vehicles, there are various state-specific taxes that still hinder their free movement. For example, every state has its own road tax that operates with its own peculiarities. There is a definite scope to make such taxes and levies uniform. The current situation is that India has the freedom of unhindered movement of capital, goods (after GST) and people. But although people are free to move, their means of movement faces impediments. Moreover, the situation only pertains to movement by roads. While GST has put the road transport sector on a level playing field with respect to rail and air transport by removing interstate entry taxes, the goods and passenger tax is still not part of GST.

Finally, it is sufficiently clear that the implementation of GST in itself is a huge success for India. It was an uphill task to develop a consensus for such a sweeping reform of indirect taxation. Yet, before passing judgements about its success, it is important to note that the structure of GST is still evolving and is in no way a finished act. Rate rationalisation is still a work in progress, and various revenue assessments of GST are, at best, indicative of a transitory phase before the dust settles.

NOTE

1. https://www.thehindubusinessline.com/opinion/columns/slate/e-way-bills-gst-goods-transport-explained/article22799543.ece (accessed 23 November 2018).

Bibliography

Adhikari, B. (2015). 'When Does Introducing a Value-Added Tax Increase Economic Efficiency? Evidence from Synthetic Control Method', Tulane University, Department of Economics, Working Papers 1524.

Aggarwal, P. (1995). *Incidence of Major Indirect Taxes in India*. New Delhi: National Institute of Public Policy and Finance.

Ahmad, E. and N. Stern (1988). 'Alternative Sources of Government Revenue: Illustrations from India, 1979–80', in D. Newbery and N. Stern (eds), *The Theory of Taxation for Developing Countries*, pp. 281–332. New York: Published for World Bank by Oxford University Press.

Annacondia, F. and W. van der Corput (2003). 'VAT Registration Thresholds in Europe', *International VAT Monitor*, 14(1): 71–72.

Artavanis, N. (2015). 'The Effect of the VAT Rate on Tax Evasion: Evidence from the Restaurant Industry in Greece', SSRN Electronic Journal. Available at SSRN: https://ssrn.com/abstract=2585147 (accessed 15 September 2018).

Bagchi, A. (2006). 'Towards GST: Choices and Trade-offs', *Economic and Political Weekly*, 41(14): 1314–1317.

——— (2007). 'International Lessons in Goods and Services Tax', *Economic and Political Weekly*, 42(45–46): 28–32.

Banerjee, S. and S. Prasad (2017). 'Small Businesses in the GST Regime', *Economic and Political Weekly*, 52(38): 18–22.

Barro, R. B. and X. Sala-i-Martin (1992). 'Public Finance in Models of Economic Growth', *The Review of Economic Studies*, 59(201): 645–662.

Besley, T. and T. Persson (2011). *Pillars of Prosperity: The Political Economics of Development Clustersq*. Princeton: Princeton University Press.

——— (2013). 'Taxation and Development', in Alan Auerbach, Raj Chetty, Martin Feldstein and Emmanuel Saez (eds), *Handbook of Public Economics*, vol. 5, pp. 51–110. Amsterdam and Oxford, UK: Elsevier.

Besley, T. and T. Persson (2014a). 'Why Do Developing Countries Tax So Little?' *Journal of Economic Perspectives*, 28(4): 99–120.

——— (2014b). 'The Causes and Consequences of Development Clusters: State Capacity, Peace and Income', *Annual Review of Economics*, 6(1): 927-949.

Bird, R. and M. Smart (2008). 'The Impact on Investment of Replacing a Retail Sales Tax by a Value-Added Tax: Evidence from Canadian Experience', Rotman Institute for International Business, Joseph L. Rotman School of Management, University of Toronto, Working Papers Series, 62.

Bird, R. and P. -P. Gendron (2001). 'VATs in Federal States: International Experience and Emerging Possibilities', Georgia State University, International Studies Program, Working Paper 01–4.

——— (2007). *The VAT in Developing and Transitional Countries*. Cambridge: Cambridge University Press.

Blazic, H. (2004). 'Tax Compliance Costs of Small Business in Croatia', Institute of Public Finance, University of Rieka, Occasional Paper 22.

Boadway, Robin, Nicolas Marceau and Steeve Mongrain (2007). 'Redistributive Taxation under Ethical Behaviour', *Scandinavian Journal of Economics*, 109(3): 505–529.

Bogetic, Z. and F. Hassan (1993). 'Determinants of Value-Added Tax Revenues: A Cross-Section Analysis', The World Bank, Policy Research Working Paper Series 1181.

Caiden, N. and A. Wildavsky (1980). *Planning and Budgeting in Poor Countries*. New Brunswick, New Jersey: Transaction Books.

Chakraborty, P. (2017). 'GST: Too Late for the Battle on Federalism and Fiscal Autonomy', NIPFP Blogs. Available at https://www.nipfp.org.in/blog/2017/05/26/gst-too-late-battle-federalism-and-fiscal-autonomy/ (accessed 26 May 2017).

Chakraborty, P., M. Gupta and L. Kaur (2017). *Analysis of State Budgets 2017–18: Emerging Issues*. New Delhi: Published by National Institute of Public Finance and Policy.

Cnossen, S. (2004). 'VAT in South Africa: What Kind of Rate Structure?' *International VAT Monitor*, 15(1): 19–24.

Comptroller and Auditor General of India (CAG). (2017). *Report of the Comptroller and Auditor General of India*, Accounts of the Union Government No. 44 of 2017 (Financial Audit). Available at https://cag.gov.in/sites/default/files/audit_report_files/Report_No.44_of_2017_-_Financial_Audit_on_Accounts_of_the_Union_Government.pdf (accessed 3 July 2018).

Denninger, S. and A. Carare (2008). 'Inflation Smoothing and the Modest Effect of VAT in Germany', International Monetary Fund (IMF), IMF Working Paper No. 08/175.

Desai, M. and J. R. Hines Jr. (2005). 'Value-Added Taxes and International Trade: The Evidence', mimeo, Michigan: University of Michigan.

Deutsche Bundesbank. (2008). *Monthly Report*, April, 60(4).

Dickinson, I. and D. White (2008). 'Tax Design Insights from the New Zealand Goods and Services Tax (GST) Model', Centre for Accounting, Governance and Taxation Research Working Paper Research Series, Working Paper No. 60.

Ebrill, L., M. Keen, J. -P. Bodin and V. Summers (2001). *The Modern VAT*. Washington, D.C.: International Monetary Fund.

The Economic Times (2017a). 'GST: Procedural Uncertainties, GSTN Issues Major Downside', 10 October 2017. Available at https://economictimes.indiatimes.com/small-biz/policy-trends/gst-procedural-uncertainties-gstn-issues-major-downside/articleshow/61016851.cms (accessed 11 June 2018).

——— (2017b). 'All Evidence Suggest Unorganized Sector, SMEs Worst Hit by Demonetization', 7 November 2017. Available at https://economictimes.indiatimes.com/small-biz/sme-sector/all-evidence-suggest-unorganised-sector-smes-worst-hit-by-demonetisation-arun-kumar/articleshow/61542781.cms (accessed 20 January 2018).

———. 2018. 'States Not in Favour of Petrol, Diesel Inclusion into GST: FM', 5 February 2018. Available at https://economictimes.indiatimes.com/news/economy/policy/states-not-in-favour-of-petrol-diesel-inclusion-into-gst-fm/articleshow/62794412.cms (accessed 11 June 2018).

Edmiston, K. and R. M. Bird (2004). 'Taxing Consumption in Jamaica: The GCT and the SCT', International Tax Program (ITP), Rotman School of Management, University of Toronto, ITP Paper 0414.

Empowered Committee of State Finance Ministers (2009). 'First Discussion Paper on Goods and Services Tax in India', New Delhi.

Emran, M. Shahe and Joseph E. Stiglitz (2005). 'On Selective Indirect Tax Reform in Developing Countries', *Journal of Public Economics*, 89(4): 599–623.

EY. (2018). *Worldwide VAT, GST and Sales Tax Guide 2018.* Ernst & Young. Available at https://www.ey.com/Publication/vwLUAssets/EY_Worldwide_VAT,_GST_and_Sales_Tax_Guide_2018/%24File/Worldwide%20VAT,%20GST%20and%20Sales%20Tax%20Guide%202018.pdf (accessed 20 June 2018).

Feldstein, Martin and Paul Krugman (1989). 'International Trade Effects of Value-Added Taxation', National Bureau of Economic Research (NBER), Cambridge, MA, NBER Working Paper Series, No. 3163.

Gallagher, M. (2005). 'Benchmarking Tax Systems', *Public Administration and Development*, 25(2): 125–144.

Gordon, Roger and Wei Li (2009). 'Tax Structures in Developing Countries: Many Puzzles and a Possible Explanation', *Journal of Public Economics*, 93(7–8): 855–866.

International Monetary Fund (IMF) (2018). 'IMF Country Report, Islamic Republic of Afghanistan'. Available at https://www.imf.org/~/media/Files/Publications/CR/2018/cr18127.ashx (accessed 17 September 2018).

International Tax Dialogue (2005). 'The Value Added Tax—Experiences and Issues', Background Paper.

Jain, R. K. (1993). *Excise and Customs Case Referencer.* New Delhi: Centax Publications.

Jeffery, O. (2011). 'Improving Performance of VAT Systems Is a Priority in the Context of the Economic Crisis', *World Commerce Review*, 5(3): 8–10.

Keen, M. (2007). 'VAT Attacks!' *International Tax and Public Finance*, 14(4): 365–381.

——— (2008). 'VAT, Tariffs, and Withholding: Border Taxes and Informality in Developing Countries', *Journal of Public Economics*, 92(10–11): 1892–1906.

——— (2013). 'The Anatomy of the VAT', International Monetary Fund (IMF), IMF Working Paper No. 3/111.

Keen, M. and B. Lockwood (2006). 'Is the VAT a Money Machine?' *National Tax Journal*, 59(4): 905–928.

——— (2007). 'The Value-Added Tax: Its Causes and Consequences', International Monetary Fund (IMF), IMF Working Paper No. 07/183.

Keen, M. and J. Mintz (2004). 'The Optimal Threshold for a Value Added Tax', *Journal of Public Economics*, 88(3–4): 559–576.

Keen, M. and M. Syed (2006). 'Domestic Taxes and International Trade: Some Evidence', International Monetary Fund (IMF), IMF Working Paper No. 06/47.

Kumar, A. (2015). 'Macroeconomic Aspects of Goods and Services Tax', *Economic and Political Weekly*, 50(29): 26–30.

Leemput, E. V. (2016). 'A Passage to India: Quantifying Internal and External Barriers to Trade', International Finance Discussion Papers 1185.

Leemput, E. V. and E. A. Wiencek (2017). 'The Effect of the GST on Indian Growth', International Finance Discussion Paper (IFDP) Notes. Washington: Board of Governors of the Federal Reserve System, 24 March 2017.

Livemint (2017). 'The Flip Side of GST: Its Impact on the Informal Economy', 22 June 2017. Available at https://www.livemint.com/Money/Hr30Wh3Bg3MAyelpa7bOXM/The-flip-side-of-GST-its-impact-on-the-informal-economy.html (accessed 15 January 2018).

Miki, B. (2011). 'The Effect of the VAT Rate Change on Aggregate Consumption and Economic Growth', Columbia Business School, Working Paper Series No. 297.

Ministry of Finance (2001). *Report of the Expert Group on Taxation of Services*. New Delhi: Ministry of Finance, Government of India.

——— (2004). *Report on the Implementation of the Fiscal Responsibility and Budget Management Act, 2003*. New Delhi: Ministry of Finance, Government of India.

——— (2012). 'Government's White Paper on Black Money', Ministry of Finance, Government of India.

——— (2015). *Report on the Revenue Neutral Rate and Structure of Rates for the Goods and Services Tax (GST)*. New Delhi: Ministry of Finance, Government of India. Available at http://www.gstcouncil.gov.in/sites/default/files/CEA-rpt-rnr.pdf (accessed 21 September 2018).

——— (2018). *Economic Survey 2017–18*. New Delhi: Ministry of Finance, Government of India.

Ministry of Finance and Company Affairs (2002). *Report of the Task Force on Indirect Taxes* (Chairman, Vijay L. Kelkar). New Delhi: Ministry of Finance and Company Affairs, Government of India.

Munk, Claus and Carsten Sorensen (2004). 'Optimal Consumption and Investment Strategies with Stochastic Interest Rates', *Journal of Banking & Finance*, 28(8): 1987–2013.

Myles, G. (2000). 'Taxation and Economic Growth', *Fiscal Studies*, 21(1): 141–168

Nair, S. R. and L. M. Eapen (2017). 'Price Monitoring and Control under GST: Lessons from Australia', *Economic and Political Weekly*, 52(25–26).

National Commission for Enterprises in the Unorganised Sector (NCEUS) (2009). *The Challenge of Employment in India: An Informal Economy Perspective*. New Delhi: National Commission for Enterprises in the Unorganised Sector.

National Council of Applied Economic Research (NCAER) (2009). *Moving to Goods and Services Tax in India: Impact on India's Growth and International Trade*. New Delhi: NCAER.

National Institute of Public Finance and Policy (NIPFP) (1994). *Reform of Domestic Trade Taxes in India: Issues and Options*. New Delhi: NIPFP.

National Statistical Commission (NSC) (2012). *Report of the Committee on Unorganised Sector Statistics*. New Delhi: National Statistical Commission.

Nellor, D. (1987). 'The Effect of the Value-Added Tax on the Tax Ratio', International Monetary Fund (IMF), IMF Working Paper No. 87/47.

Organisation for Economic Co-Operation and Development (OECD) (2003). *Report on the Use of Simplified Registration Systems*, Committee on Fiscal Affairs, DAFFE/CF (2003)43/ANN4, July.

——— (2004a). *Consumption Tax Trends*. Paris: OECD Publishing.

——— (2004b). *Tax Administration in OECD Countries: Comparative Information Series*. Centre for Tax Policy and Administration.

——— (2006). *Centre for Tax Policy and Administration Tax Administration in OECD and Selected Non-OECD*. Paris: OECD Publishing.

——— (2010). *Tax Policy Reform and Economic Growth*. OECD Tax Policy Studies, No. 20. Paris: OECD Publishing.

——— (2011). *Consumption Tax Trends 2010: VAT/GST and Excise Rates, Trends and Administration Issues*. Paris: OECD Publishing

Patnaik, Prabhat (2017). 'Strangulating the Informal Economy', *Frontline*, 24 October 2017. Available at http://www.frontline.in/cover-story/strangulating-the-informal-economy/article9896607.ece (accessed 15 January 2018).

Piggott, John and John Whalley (2001). 'VAT Base Broadening, Self Supply, and the Informal Sector', *American Economic Review*, 91(4): 1084–1094.

Pomeranz, D. (2015). 'No Taxation without Information: Deterrence and Self-Enforcement in the Value Added Tax', *American Economic Review*, 105(8): 2539–2569.

Public Finance Public Accountability Collective (PFPAC) (2017). 'GST: Impact on Small Industry and the Informal Sector'. Public Finance Public Accountability Collective. Available at https://pfpacjournal.blogspot.in/2017/09/gst-impact-on-small-industry-and.html (accessed 15 January 2018).

Rao, K. and P. Chakraborty (2010). 'Goods and Services Tax in India: An Assessment of the Base', *Economic and Political Weekly*, 45(1): 49–54.

Reserve Bank of India (RBI) (2017a). 'Bi-Monthly Monetary Policy Committee Statement', December, Reserve Bank of India. Available at https://rbi.org.in/Scripts/BS_PressReleaseDisplay.aspx?prid=45656 (accessed 11 September 2018).

——— (2017b). *Monetary Policy Report*. Available at https://rbi.org.in/scripts/PublicationsView.aspx?id=18027#BX21 (accessed 23 July 2018).

——— (2018a). *Annual Report 2017–18*. Reserve Bank of India.

——— (2018b). 'Bi-Monthly Monetary Policy Committee Statement', February, Reserve Bank of India. Available at https://rbi.org.in/Scripts/BS_PressReleaseDisplay.aspx?prid=45656 (accessed 11 September 2018).

Ruebling, C. (1973). 'A Value Added Tax and Factors Affecting its Economic Impact', *Federal Reserve Bank of St. Louis Review*, 55(9): 15–19.

Sandford, C. (2000). *Why Tax Systems Differ: A Comparative Study of the Political Economy of Taxation*. Bath: Fiscal Publications.

Sandford, C. and J. Hasseldine (1992). *The Complaince Costs of Business Taxes in New Zealand*. Wellington: Institute of Policy Studies, Victoria University of Wellington.

Shang, L. K. and G. H. Leng (2014). 'GST in Singapore and Malaysia', *International Tax Review*. Available at https://www.internationaltaxreview.com/Article/3386119/GST-in-Singapore-and-Malaysia.html (accessed 16 August 2018).

Silvani, C. and P. dos Santos (1996). 'Administrative Aspects of Brazil's Consumption Tax Reform', *International VAT Monitor*, 7: 123–132.

Sinn, H.-W., A. Gebauer and R. Parsche (2004). 'The IFO Institute's Model for Reducing VAT Fraud: Payment First, Refund Later', *CESifo Forum*, 5(2): 30–34.

T. N. Ninan. (2017). 'A Bone in the Throat', *Business Standard*, 27 November 2017. Available at http://www.business-standard.com/article/opinion/t-n-ninan-a-bone-in-the-throat-117112400728_1.html (accessed 15 January 2018).

Tait, A. (1988). *Value Added Tax: International Practice and Problems*. Washington, D.C.: International Monetary Fund.

The Constitution (One Hundred And Twenty-Second Amendment) Bill, 2014. Available at https://rajyasabha.nic.in/rsnew/122nd_bill.pdf (accessed 17 June 2018).

The Hindu Business Line (2018). 'All You Wanted to Know about E-way Bill', 19 February 2018. Available at https://www.thehindubusinessline.com/opinion/columns/slate/e-way-bills-gst-goods-transport-explained/article22799543.ece (accessed 14 March 2018).

Thirteenth Finance Commission (2009). *Report on the Task Force on Goods and Services Tax*. Available at https://www.prsindia.org/sites/default/files/bill_files/Report_of_Task_Force-_GST.pdf (accessed 11 September 2018).

Tomar, S., S. Mathur and S. Ghosh (2018). 'Working Capital Constraints and Exports: Evidence from the GST Rollout', Mint Street Memo No. 10, Reserve Bank of India.

Vaidya, D. S. and K. Kanagasabapathy (2013). 'Reform of Indirect Taxes—Hurdles before the GST', *Economic and Political Weekly*, 48(26–27): 79–81.

Valadkhani, A. and A. Layton (2004). 'Quantifying the Effect of GST on Inflation in Australia's Capital Cities: An Intervention Analysis', *Australian Economic Review*, 37(2): 125–138.

Wittwer, G. and K. Anderson (2001). 'Impact of Tax Reform on the Australian Wine Industry: A CGE Analysis', Centre for International Economic Studies, Discussion Paper No. 9908.

Wong and Partners (2016). 'GST in Malaysia—One Year On'. Available at https://www.bakermckenzie.com/-/media/files/insight/publications/2016/04/gst-in-malaysia-one-year-on/al_kulalumpur_gstmalaysia_apr16.pdf?la=en (accessed 23 August 2018).

World Bank (2018) *India Development Update: India's Growth Story*. Available at http://documents.worldbank.org/curated/

en/814101517840592525/pdf/123152-REVISED-PUBLIC-MARCH14-IDU-March-2018-with-cover-page.pdf (accessed 2 April 2018).

Zhou, L. Z., J. Tam and J. Heng-Contaxis (2013). 'The Introduction of Goods and Services Tax in Malaysia: A Policy Analysis', Centre for Public Policy Studies (CPPS) Policy Paper Series, Asian Strategy & Leadership Institute.

Index